The Awesome Amazing Quiz Book Table Of Contents

Answers

Movies

1. 1970s Movies

1. Who directed the movie The Godfather?

2. Which movie features the iconic line, "I'm as mad as hell, and I'm not going to take this anymore!"?

3. Who played the character of "Rocky Balboa" in the movie Rocky?

4. In which 1979 movie does Sigourney Weaver play the character of "Ripley"?

5. Which 1973 movie tells the story of a young woman's journey of self-discovery and sexual liberation?

6. Who played the character of "Don Vito Corleone" in the movie The Godfather?

7, Which movie stars Robert De Niro as a young Vito Corleone?

8. Which 1995 movie features the song "Bohemian Rhapsody" by Queen?

9. Who directed the movie Star Wars: A New Hope?

10. Which 1971 movie tells the story of a detective who becomes obsessed with a case involving a small-time criminal and his girlfriend?

11. Which movie features John Travolta as a working-class young man who dreams of becoming a disco king?

12. Who played the character of "Luke Skywalker" in the movie Star Wars: A New Hope?

13. Which movie stars Gene Hackman as a detective who gets caught up in a dangerous conspiracy involving the French police?

14. In which movie does Al Pacino play the character of "Tony Montana", a Cuban immigrant who rises to the top of a drug cartel?

15. Which movie tells the story of a group of friends who travel to Amity Island to hunt a killer shark?

16. Who directed the movie Apocalypse Now?

17. Which movie features Richard Dreyfuss as a man who becomes obsessed with UFO sightings?

18. In which movie does Robert De Niro play the character of "Travis Bickle", a disturbed taxi driver in New York City?

19. Which movie stars Jack Nicholson as a private investigator who becomes embroiled in a complex mystery in 1930s Los Angeles?

20. Who directed the 1973 movie The Exorcist?

2. 1980s Movies

1. In "Back to the Future," what is the name of the time machine?

2. What was the name of the computer in "WarGames"?

3. Who played the character of Indiana Jones in "Raiders of the Lost Ark"?

4. What was the name of the character played by Molly Ringwald in "The Breakfast Club"?

5. In "E.T. the Extra-Terrestrial," what is the name of the actress who plays Eliot's little sister, Gertie Taylor?

6. What is the name of the dance that Kevin Bacon's character does in "Footloose"?

7. In "The Princess Bride," what is the name of the character played by Mandy Patinkin?

8. What is the name of the character played by Tom Hanks in "Big"?

9. Who played the character of Axel Foley in "Beverly Hills Cop"?

10. In "Top Gun," what is the call sign of Tom Cruise's character?

11. What is the name of the high school that the characters in "Ferris Bueller's Day Off" attend?

12. Who played the character of John McClane in "Die Hard"?

13. What was the name of the character played by Sigourney Weaver in "Aliens"?

14. In "The Karate Kid," what is the name of the karate teacher played by Pat Morita?

15. Who played the character of Marty McFly in "Back to the Future"?

16. What is the model number of the character played by Arnold Schwarzenegger in "The Terminator"?

17. What was the name of the character played by Sean Astin in "The Goonies"?

18. Who played the character of Robocop in the 1987 movie?

19. In "The NeverEnding Story," what is the name of the luck dragon?

20. Who played the character of the Wicked Witch of the West in "The Wizard of Oz" prequel "Return to Oz" (1985)?

3. 1990s Movies

1. What was the name of the actress who played Rose Dewitt in "Titanic?

2. What was the name of the character played by Gary Sinise in "Forrest Gump"?

3. Who played the character of Clarice Starling in "The Silence of the Lambs"?

4. In "Jurassic Park," what was the name of the island where the dinosaurs were kept?

5. What was the name of the character played by Robin Williams in "Mrs. Doubtfire"?

6. In "Pulp Fiction," what was the name of the character played by John Travolta?

7. Who played the character of Jack Dawson in "Titanic"?

8. In "The Lion King," what was the name of Simba's father?

9. What was the name of the character played by Keanu Reeves in "The Matrix"?

10. Who played the character of Andy Dufresne in "The Shawshank Redemption"?

11. What was the name of the character played by Will Smith in "Independence Day"?

12. Who played the character of Edward Scissorhands in the 1990 movie?

13. In "Clueless," what was the name of the character played by Alicia Silverstone?

14. Who played the character of Annie Wilkes in "Misery"?

15. In "Dumb and Dumber," what was the name of the character played by Jim Carrey?

16. What was the name of the character played by Emma Thompson in "Sense and Sensibility"?

17. In "Terminator 2: Judgment Day," what is the name of the liquid metal robot that tries to kill John Connor?

18. Who played the character of Hannibal Lecter in "The Silence of the Lambs"?

19. What was the name of the character played by Drew Barrymore in "Scream"?

20. Who directed the 1991 movie "Beauty and the Beast"?

4. 2000s Movies

1. What was the title of the first film in the "Lord of the Rings" trilogy?

2. In the movie "Mean Girls," what is the name of the high school attended by the main character, Cady Heron?

3. Who played the character of Jack Sparrow in the "Pirates of the Caribbean" series?

4. What was the name of the character played by Heath Ledger in "Brokeback Mountain"?

5. In "The Dark Knight," what was the name of the character played by Heath Ledger?

6. Who played the character of Neo in "The Matrix" sequels?

7. What was the name of the character played by Ellen Page in "Juno"?

8. In "Spider-Man," what was the name of the character played by Willem Dafoe?

9. Who directed the 2004 movie "Eternal Sunshine of the Spotless Mind"?

10. What was the name of the character played by Jamie Foxx in "Ray"?

11. Who played the character of Gollum in "The Lord of the Rings" trilogy?

12. In "Harry Potter and the Philosopher's Stone," what is the name of the game played on broomsticks?

13. What was the name of the character played by Hilary Swank in "Million Dollar Baby"?

14. In "The Da Vinci Code," what was the name of the character played by Tom Hanks?

15. Who played the character of Borat Sagdiyev in the 2006 movie "Borat"?

16. What was the name of the character played by Naomi Watts in "Mulholland Drive"?

17. In "The Bourne Identity," what was the name of the character played by Matt Damon?

18. Who played the character of Captain Jack Aubrey in the 2003 movie "Master and Commander: The Far Side of the World"?

19. In "The Incredibles," what is the name of the superhero family at the center of the story?

20. Who directed the 2000 movie "Gladiator"?

5. 2010s Movies

1. What was the name of the character played by Eddie Redmayne in "The Theory of Everything"?

2. Who played the character of Joy in the movie "Inside Out"?

3. What was the name of the character played by Emma Stone in "La La Land"?

4. In the movie "The Social Network," who played the character of Mark Zuckerberg?

5. Who played the character of Katniss Everdeen in the "Hunger Games" movies?

6. In "The Martian," what was the name of the character played by Matt Damon?

7. Who directed the 2017 movie "Get Out"?

8. What was the full name of the character played by Saoirse Ronan in "Lady Bird"?

9. In "Black Panther," what is the name of the kingdom ruled by T'Challa?

10. Who played the character of Tony Stark/Iron Man in the Marvel Cinematic Universe?

11. In "Frozen," what was the name of the character voiced by Idina Menzel?

12. Who played the character of Rey in the "Star Wars" sequel trilogy?

13. What was the name of the character played by Leonardo DiCaprio in "The Wolf of Wall Street"?

14. In "The Shape of Water," what was the name of the creature played by Doug Jones?

15. Who played the character of Arthur Fleck in "Joker"?

16. What was the name of the character played by Tom Holland in "Spider-Man: Homecoming"?

17. In "Interstellar," what was the name of the spaceship piloted by Matthew McConaughey's character?

18. Who directed the 2013 movie "Gravity"?

19. What was the name of the character played by Daniel Kaluuya in the movie "Black Panther"?

20. In "Toy Story 3," what is the name of the daycare center where Woody and the other toys end up?

TV

6. 1980s TV Shows

1. In "The A-Team," what was the name of the team's leader?

2. What was the name of the robot that was one of the main characters in "Small Wonder"?

3. What was the profession of Angela Bower, one of the main characters in "Who's the Boss?"?

4. In "Cheers," what was the name of the bar's owner?

5. What was the first name of the character played by Tom Selleck in "Magnum, P.I."?

6. What was the name of the high school in "Saved by the Bell"?

7. In "Knight Rider," what was the name of the car that was the main character's sidekick?

8. What was the name of the family in "Family Ties"?

9. What was the name of the character played by Michael J. Fox in "Family Ties"?

10. What was the name of the character played by Alyssa Milano in "Who's the Boss?"?

11. What was the name of the high school in "Fame"?

12. What was the name of the family in "The Cosby Show"?

13. What was the name of the character played by Tony Danza in "Who's the Boss?"?

14. In "The Golden Girls," what was the name of the character played by Betty White?

15. What was the name of the character played by Michael Gross in "Family Ties"?

16. What was the name of the character played by Gary Coleman in "Diff'rent Strokes"?

17. What was the name of the character played by Bruce Willis in "Moonlighting"?

18. What was the name of the high school in "21 Jump Street"?

19. In "The Facts of Life," what was the name of the school the characters attended?

20. What was the name of the character played by John Stamos in "Full House"?

7. 1990s TV shows

19. What was the name of the family on the TV show "The Simpsons"?

20. Who played the character of Liz Lemon on the TV show "30 Rock"?

9. Cartoon Characters

1. What is the name of the father character in the animated TV show "The Simpsons"?

2. Who is the famous rabbit character who always says "What's up, Doc?"?

3. What is the name of the character who is the arch-nemesis of Batman in the animated series "Batman: The Animated Series"?

4. Who is the character who is always chasing after the elusive "Road Runner" in the animated TV show "Looney Tunes"?

5. What is the name of the main character in the animated movie "Finding Nemo"?

6. Who is the character in the animated movie "The Lion King" who sings the song "Hakuna Matata"?

7. What is the name of the character who is always causing trouble for the other characters in the animated TV show "Tom and Jerry"?

8. Who is the character who is a yellow, sponge-like creature who lives in a pineapple under the sea?

9. What is the name of the character who is the sidekick to the superhero "Superman" in the animated TV show "Super Friends"?

10. Who is the character who is always trying to catch the mischievous "Jerry" in the animated TV show "Tom and Jerry"?

Video Games

10. 1990s Video Games

1. What is the name of the villain character in the game "Super Mario 64"?

2. What is the name of the protagonist in the game "The Legend of Zelda: Ocarina of Time"?

3. What is the name of the villain in the game "Sonic the Hedgehog"?

4. What is the name of the first-person shooter game released in 1993 that revolutionized the genre?

5. What is the name of the racing game that features characters from the Mario franchise?
t 64.
6. What is the name of the adventure game that follows the story of a young boy named Ness?

7. What is the name of the puzzle game that was created by a Russian scientist named Alexey Pajitnov?

8. What is the name of the 1995 game that features a green dinosaur named Yoshi as Mario's sidekick?

9. What is the name of the fighting game from 1991 that featured characters named Ken and Ryu and popularized the fighting genre?

10. What is the name of the game that features a yellow creature named Pikachu and launched the Pokemon franchise?

11. What is the name of the platform game that features a bandicoot named Crash as the protagonist?

12. What is the name of the game that features a genetically enhanced soldier named Solid Snake?

13. What is the name of the game that features Lara Croft as the protagonist?

14. What is the name of the game that features a gorilla named Donkey Kong as the protagonist?

15. What is the name of the role-playing game that follows the story of Cloud Strife?

16. What is the name of the game that features a plumber named Luigi as Mario's brother?

17. What is the name of the 1998 game that features a blue hedgehog named Sonic as the protagonist?

18. What is the name of the game that follows the adventures of an astronaut named Roger Wilco?

19. What is the name of the game that features an alien named Abe as the protagonist?

20. What is the name of the game that features a prince named Raziel as the protagonist?

11. 2000s Video Games

1. What is the name of the game that features a silent protagonist named Gordon Freeman and introduces the "Gravity Gun"?

2. What is the name of the game that follows the story of a Spartan soldier named Master Chief?

3. What is the name of the game that is based on a 1995 game and released on Nintendo DS in 2008 that features a group of kids who travel through time to save the world from a monster?

.4. What is the name of the game that features a black ops soldier named Alex Mason?

5. What is the name of the game that features an assassin named Altair?

6. What is the name of the game that features a survivor named Leon Kennedy and a police officer named Claire Redfield?

7. What is the name of the game that follows the story of a boy who becomes a Pokemon Trainer and tries to catch all the Pokemon?

8. What is the name of the game that features a character named Kratos and is based on Greek mythology?

9. What is the name of the game that features a protagonist named Jack and a battle royale on an island?

10. What is the name of the game that follows the story of an adventurer named Nathan Drake?

11. What is the name of the game that features a character named John Marston and is set in the Wild West?

12. What is the name of the game that features a plumber named Mario and introduced the "FLUDD" device?

13. What is the name of the 2006 game that follows the story of a young woman named Lara Croft?

14. What is the name of the game that features a group of soldiers fighting against a parasitic race?

15. What is the name of the game that features a protagonist named Ratchet and his robotic sidekick named Clank?

16. What is the name of the game that features a protagonist named Vincent Valentine and takes place in the same universe as Final Fantasy VII?

17. What is the name of the game that features a character named Dante and his demon-hunting adventures?

18. What is the name of the game that features a protagonist named Marcus Fenix and is set in a post-apocalyptic world?

19. What is the name of the game that features a protagonist named Sora and his journey to save multiple worlds?

20. What is the name of the game that features a character named Ezio Auditore da Firenze and is set in Renaissance Italy?

Comic Books

12. Comic Book Characters

1. Who is the alter ego of Spider-Man?

2. What is the real name of Batman?

3. Who is the villain who can control metal in the X-Men series?

4. What is the name of the planet Superman comes from?

5. Who is the archenemy of the Flash?

6. What is the name of the primary villain in the Fantastic Four?

7. Who is the love interest of Tony Stark in the Iron Man comics?

8. What is the name of the antihero who first appeared in Todd McFarlane's Spider-Man comic?

9. Who is the creator of the Watchmen comics?

10. What is the real name of the Green Lantern?

11. Who is the archenemy of Batman in the comics?

12. What is the name of the comic book character who wields Mjolnir?

13. Who is the leader of the X-Men?

14. Who is the love interest of Peter Parker in the Spider-Man comics?

15. What is the real name of Captain America?

16. Who is the main villain in the Daredevil comics?

17. What is the name of the symbiote that bonds with Eddie Brock to create Venom?

18. Who is the archenemy of the Teenage Mutant Ninja Turtles?

19. What is the name of the comic book character who is blind but has heightened senses?

20. Who is the archenemy of the Avengers?

13. Comic Book Superheroes And Their Abilities - Answer the questions by giving the name of the superhero who matches the given abilities.

1. Super strength, speed, and durability; heat vision, freeze breath, and x-ray vision

2. Peak human strength and agility, martial arts skills, and a variety of gadgets and vehicles

3. Superhuman strength, agility, and reflexes; spider-sense and the ability to cling to surfaces

4. Powered armor with enhanced strength and weapons, including repulsor beams and missiles

5. Super strength and durability, the power of flight, and the ability to deflect projectiles with her bracelets

6. Peak human strength, speed, and agility; expert martial artist and strategist

7. Superhuman strength and durability, control over lightning and storms, and the ability to fly with his hammer

8. Super strength and durability that increases as he becomes angrier; the ability to jump great distances and cause earthquakes

9. Adamantium-laced skeleton and claws, enhanced senses, and a rapid healing factor

10. Superhuman speed and agility, the ability to vibrate through solid objects and travel through time

11. Super strength, durability, and swimming speed; the ability to communicate with sea creatures

12. Power ring that creates constructs out of green light and provides flight and a protective force field

13. Peak human strength, agility, and martial arts skills; expert spy and assassin

14. Mastery of magic, including astral projection, teleportation, and the ability to manipulate reality

15. Superhuman senses and agility; expert martial artist and acrobat

16. Optic blasts that can level buildings and a visor to control them; leadership skills as the leader of the X-Men

17. Control over weather and the ability to fly; a skilled fighter and leader

18. Super strength and durability, a rocky exterior that provides protection, and a skilled pilot

19. Ability to shrink and grow in size, and communicate with insects; a suit that allows him to control ants and other bugs

20. Peak human strength and endurance, expert marksman and hand-to-hand fighter

21. Reality-warping powers that allow her to manipulate probability and time

22. Peak human strength and agility, martial arts skills, and a variety of gadgets and vehicles

23. Ability to transform into a superhero with the powers of six Greek gods: wisdom, strength, stamina, power, courage, and speed

24. Master archer and hand-to-hand fighter, skilled tactician and strategist

25. Ability to absorb the memories, powers, and abilities of others through touch

26. Super strength and durability, the ability to communicate with supernatural creatures, and a variety of weapons and gadgets

27. Power cosmic that grants him superhuman strength, speed, and durability, the ability to fly through space and manipulate energy

28. Super strength and agility, expert swordsman, and a vampire hunter with immunity to their bites

29. Superhuman strength, agility, and senses, and mastery of Vibranium technology

30. Telepathic and telekinetic powers that allow her to read minds and move objects with her thoughts; one of the most powerful mutants in the X-Men universe

History

14. Ancient Egyptians

1. What was the ancient Egyptian writing system called?

2. Who was the famous female pharaoh of ancient Egypt?

3. What is the name of the ancient Egyptian god of the afterlife?

4. Which river was the ancient Egyptian civilization centered around?

5. What is the name of the famous tomb where King Tutankhamun was buried?

6. What is the name of the ancient Egyptian sun god?

7. What is the name of the process of preserving a body for the afterlife?

8. What is the name of the ancient Egyptian cat goddess?

9. What is the name of the ancient Egyptian symbol of protection that is often depicted as a cross with a loop at the top?

10. What is the name of the ancient Egyptian god of the sky and kingship?

11. What is the name of the ancient Egyptian god of wisdom and writing?

12. What is the name of the ancient Egyptian goddess of fertility and motherhood?

13. What is the name of the ancient Egyptian goddess of war and hunting?

14. What is the name of the ancient Egyptian god of chaos and the desert?

15. What is the name of the ancient Egyptian god of the underworld?

16. What is the name of the ancient Egyptian queen who ruled as a pharaoh in her own right?

17. What is the name of the ancient Egyptian god of the Nile River?

18. What is the name of the ancient Egyptian god of the dead and embalming?

19. What is the name of the ancient Egyptian god of fertility and agriculture?

20. What is the name of the ancient Egyptian god of the sun and creation?

15. Ancient China

1. Who was the first emperor of China?

2. What is the name of the famous wall built by the Chinese?

3. What is the name of the dynasty that ruled China during the height of the Silk Road trade?

4. What is the name of the famous explorer who traveled the world in the early 15th century and visited China?

5. What is the name of the famous philosopher and author who wrote The Art of War?

6. Who was the only female emperor of China?

7. What is the name of the Chinese philosopher who is famous for his teachings on Confucianism?

8. What is the name of the Chinese festival that celebrates the start of the lunar new year?

9. What is the name of the famous garden in Suzhou, China, that is known for its classical Chinese garden design?

10. What is the name of the ancient trade route that connected China to the Mediterranean world?

11. What is the name of the Chinese religion that combines elements of Buddhism, Taoism, and Confucianism?

12. What is the name of the famous Chinese poet who lived during the Tang Dynasty and wrote about nature and romance?

13. What is the name of the famous Chinese instrument that is played with a bow and is often featured in Chinese music?

14. What is the name of the Chinese martial art that is known for its slow, flowing movements and is often practiced for health and meditation?

15. What is the name of the Chinese emperor who commissioned the construction of the Forbidden City?

16. What is the name of the ancient Chinese writing system that uses characters instead of an alphabet?

17. What is the name of the Chinese tea ceremony that emphasizes mindfulness and focus?

18. What is the name of the Chinese festival that celebrates the annual autumn harvest?

19. What is the name of the famous Chinese novel that tells the story of a young man's journey to becoming a powerful warrior?

20. What is the name of the famous Chinese calligrapher who lived during the Tang Dynasty and is known for his bold and expressive style?

16. The Revolutionary War

1. In what year did the American Revolutionary War begin?

2. Which document declared the 13 British colonies in North America to be free and independent states?

3. Who was the commander-in-chief of the Continental Army during the Revolutionary War?

4. What was the name of the battle that was the turning point of the Revolutionary War, and led to France's support of the American cause?

5. What was the name of the British general who surrendered his army at the Battle of Yorktown, effectively ending the Revolutionary War?

6. Who wrote the pamphlet "Common Sense," which was widely read in the American colonies and helped to inspire support for independence from Britain?

7. What was the name of the treaty that ended the Revolutionary War and recognized the independence of the United States?

8. What was the name of the American Revolutionary War spy ring that was led by George Washington?

9. What was the name of the German mercenaries hired by the British to fight against the Americans in the Revolutionary War?

10. What was the name of the American naval commander who famously said, "I have not yet begun to fight!" during a naval battle in the Revolutionary War?

17. The French And Indian War

1. When did the French and Indian War begin?

2. Who was the commander of British forces in North America during the French and Indian War?

3. What was the major cause of the French and Indian War?

4. What was the name of the fort that the French built at the confluence of the Allegheny and Monongahela Rivers?

5. What was the name of the British fort that George Washington built in 1754?

6. Who was the leader of the Ottawa Indians during the French and Indian War?

7. What treaty ended the French and Indian War?

8. Which major city did the British capture in 1759, dealing a significant blow to French power in North America?

9. Who was the British Prime Minister during the French and Indian War?

10. What was the name of the first major battle of the French and Indian War, which took place in 1755?

11. Who was the commander of the French forces in North America during the French and Indian War?

12. Which Native American tribe sided with the British during the French and Indian War?

13. What was the name of the British general who was killed at the Battle of Ticonderoga in 1758?

14. What was the name of the British general who replaced General Braddock after his defeat in 1755?

15. Which future US president served as a colonel in the Virginia Regiment during the French and Indian War?

16. What was the name of the British general who captured Fort Frontenac in 1758?

17. Which French commander surrendered to the British at the Battle of Quebec in 1759?

18. What was the name of the French fort that was captured by the British in 1758, giving them control of the Great Lakes?

19. Who was the British general who defeated the French at the Battle of the Plains of Abraham in 1759?

20/ Which major North American river did the French and British fight over during the French and Indian War?

18. The Civil War

1. In what year did the Civil War begin?

2. Who was the President of the Confederate States of America?

3. Who was the President of the United States during the Civil War?

4. What was the name of the Confederate general who led the Army of Northern Virginia?

5. What was the name of the Union general who led the Army of the Potomac?

6. What was the first major battle of the Civil War?

7. What was the name of the famous speech given by President Lincoln during the Civil War?

8. What was the bloodiest one-day battle of the Civil War?

9. What was the name of the Confederate submarine that sank the Union ship Housatonic?

10. What was the name of the famous Union general who led the March to the Sea?

11. What was the name of the Confederate prison camp known for its terrible conditions?

12. Who was the Confederate general who famously surrendered at Appomattox Courthouse?

13. What was the name of the Union general who became the 18th President of the United States?

14. What was the name of the Union general who famously said "War is hell"?

15. What was the name of the Confederate general who led the raid on Harpers Ferry?

16. What was the name of the Union nurse who founded the American Red Cross?

17. What was the name of the Union general who was assassinated just days after Lee's surrender?

18. What was the name of the Confederate general who famously refused to surrender after the war had ended?

19. What was the name of the Confederate ironclad that fought the USS Monitor?

20. What was the name of the Union general who famously said "I shall return"?

19. World War 1

1. In what year did World War 1 begin?

2. What was the name of the alliance that Germany, Austria-Hungary, and Italy formed before the war?

3. What was the name of the alliance that Great Britain, France, and Russia formed before the war?

4. What was the name of the German plan to quickly defeat France before turning their attention to Russia?

5. What was the name of the ship that was sunk by a German U-boat, which helped bring the United States into the war?

6. What was the name of the peace treaty that ended World War I?

7. What was the name of the Serbian nationalist who assassinated Archduke Franz Ferdinand of Austria-Hungary, setting off the chain of events that led to war?

8. What was the name of the battle in which Germany first used poison gas?

9. What was the name of the last German offensive of the war?

10. What was the name of the battle in which the British and French armies stopped the German advance towards Paris?

11. What was the name of the American general who led the American Expeditionary Force in Europe?

12. What was the name of the airplane pilot who became the top flying ace of the war?

13. What was the name of the British nurse who founded the first professional training school for nurses during the war?

14. What was the name of the treaty that ended the war between Russia and Germany?

15. What was the name of the battle in which the British suffered their worst single-day casualties in history?

16. What was the name of the German battleship that was sunk in 1916, leading to the slogan "Remember the Maine, remember the Lusitania"?

17. What was the name of the battle in which the United States Marines first saw combat in World War I?

18. What was the name of the famous poem written by John McCrae, which is often associated with Remembrance Day?

19. What was the name of the Russian mystic who had a large influence on the Russian royal family before the war?

20. What was the name of the treaty that recognized the independence of Poland, Czechoslovakia, and Yugoslavia after the war?

20. World War 2

1. In what year did World War II begin?

2. What was the name of the German leader who led the Nazi Party during the war?

3. What was the name of the policy that the Western powers pursued towards Germany before the war?

4. What was the name of the pact that Germany and the Soviet Union signed before the war?

5. What was the name of the battle that marked the turning point on the Eastern Front of the war?

6. What was the name of the battle in which the United States Navy decisively defeated the Japanese Navy?

7. What was the name of the code-breaking machine that the British used to decode German messages during the war?

8. What was the name of the conference at which the Allied leaders discussed the post-war world?

9. What was the name of the Nazi extermination camp where over one million Jews were killed during the war?

10. What was the name of the battle in which the United States and its allies landed in Normandy to begin the liberation of Europe?

11. What was the name of the battle in which the Soviet Union defeated the German army in the largest tank battle in history?

12. What was the code name for the Manhattan Project, which developed the atomic bomb?

13. What was the name of the famous photograph taken of American Marines raising the flag on Iwo Jima?

14. What was the name of the German air force during the war?

15. What was the name of the battle in which the Soviet Union finally defeated the German army, leading to the end of the war in Europe?

16. What was the name of the treaty that ended the war between Japan and the United States?

17. What was the name of the British Prime Minister who led the country through most of the war?

18. What was the name of the Japanese emperor during the war?

19. What was the name of the battle in which the United States Marines raised the American flag on the island of Iwo Jima?

20. What was the name of the conference at which the Allied leaders decided to divide Germany into four occupation zones after the war?

21. The Vietnam War

1. In what year did the Vietnam War begin?

2. What was the name of the communist group in Vietnam that the United States fought against?

3. What was the name of the Gulf of Tonkin Resolution that gave President Lyndon B. Johnson the authority to escalate U.S. involvement in the war?

4. What was the name of the U.S. military strategy in Vietnam that involved search and destroy missions?

5. What was the name of the communist leader of North Vietnam?

6. What was the name of the U.S. Army officer who leaked the Pentagon Papers, a top-secret study of U.S. involvement in the war?

7. What was the name of the event in which unarmed Vietnamese civilians were killed by U.S. soldiers?

8. What was the name of the chemical agent that the United States used to defoliate the jungles of Vietnam?

9. What was the name of the battle in which U.S. troops fought a North Vietnamese Army division to a standstill?

10. What was the name of the U.S. Army officer who led the first major ground combat unit in Vietnam?

11. What was the name of the U.S. Marine Corps officer who won the Medal of Honor for his actions during the Battle of Hue?

12. What was the name of the U.S. Army helicopter pilot who was captured and held as a prisoner of war for over five years?

13. What was the name of the U.S. Army officer who became a vocal critic of the war and wrote the book "Dispatches"?

14. What was the name of the U.S. Army medic who refused to carry a weapon and was awarded the Medal of Honor for his bravery in saving wounded soldiers?

15. What was the name of the U.S. Army officer who led the 1st Infantry Division during the Battle of Hamburger Hill?

16. What was the name of the battle in which U.S. troops fought against the North Vietnamese Army in the Ia Drang Valley?

17. What was the name of the South Vietnamese leader who was overthrown by a military coup in 1963?

18. What was the name of the U.S. Marine Corps officer who famously declared that he had to destroy a village in order to save it?

19. What was the name of the U.S. Army helicopter pilot who was awarded the Medal of Honor for his heroism during the Battle of Ia Drang?

20. What was the name of the treaty that ended the war and led to the withdrawal of U.S. troops from Vietnam?

22. US Presidents And The Time They Served - Answer the questions by giving the year or span of years that the United States president named served as president. The first one has been done for you.

1. George Washington 1789 - 1797

2. John Adams

3. Thomas Jefferson

4. James Madison

5. James Monroe

6. John Quincy Adams

7. Andrew Jackson

8. Martin Van Buren

9. William Henry Harrison

10. John Tyler

11. James K. Polk

12. Zachary Taylor

13. Millard Fillmore

14. Franklin Pierce

15. James Buchanan

16. Abraham Lincoln

17. Andrew Johnson

18. Ulysses S. Grant

19. Rutherford B. Hayes

20. James A. Garfield

21. Woodrow Wilson

22. Warren G. Harding

23. Calvin Coolidge

24. Herbert Hoover

25. Harry S. Truman

26. Dwight D. Eisenhower 2

27. John F. Kennedy

28. Lyndon B. Johnson

29. Richard Nixon

30. Gerald Ford

People

23. Famous Artists And Their Work - Answer the questions by giving the name of the artist who created the named pieces of artwork.

1. "Mona Lisa" and "The Last Supper"

2. "David" and the Sistine Chapel ceiling

3. "Starry Night" and "Sunflowers"

4. "Les Demoiselles d'Avignon" and "Guernica"

5. "The Night Watch" and "Self-Portrait with Two Circles"

6. "Girl with a Pearl Earring" and "The Milkmaid"

7. "Water Lilies" and "Impression, Sunrise"

8. "The Persistence of Memory" and "The Elephants"

9. "The Scream" and "Madonna"

10. "The Thinker" and "The Kiss"

11. "Composition VII" and "Black and Violet"

12. "Jimson Weed" and "Red Canna"

13. "The Dance" and "The Red Studio"

14. "The Birth of Venus" and "Primavera"

15. "Number 1, 1950 (Lavender Mist)" and "Convergence"

16. "Mont Sainte-Victoire" and "The Bathers"

17. "The Kiss" and "Portrait of Adele Bloch-Bauer I"

18. "Nighthawks" and "Morning Sun"

19. "I and the Village" and "The Fiddler"

20. "The Two Fridas" and "Self-Portrait with Thorn Necklace and Hummingbird"

24. Famous Songs And Their Creators - Answer the questions by giving the name of the person or people who created the named pieces of music. The answers may be different from the band or artist who is known for performing that piece of music.

1. Bohemian Rhapsody"

2. "Stairway to Heaven"

3. "Like a Rolling Stone"

4. "Smells Like Teen Spirit"

5. "Hey Jude"

6. "Purple Haze"

7. "Imagine"

8. "Sweet Child o' Mine"

9. "Billie Jean"

10. "I Will Always Love You"

11. "Hotel California"

12. "Thriller"

13. "The Sound of Silence"

14. "My Heart Will Go On"

15. "Take on Me"

16. "Satisfaction"

17. "Hallelujah"

18. "Yesterday"

19. "Under Pressure"

25. Famous Poems And Their Authors - Answer the questions by giving the name of the author who wrote the named poem.

1. "The Waste Land"

2. "Howl"

3. "Ode to a Grecian Urn"

4. "Do Not Go Gentle into That Good Night"

5. "The Road Not Taken"

6. "Annabel Lee"

7. "The Raven"

8. "The Tyger"

9. "Ode to a Nightingale"

10. "Sonnet 18"

11. "If—"

12. "The Charge of the Light Brigade"

13. "Ozymandias"

14. "To His Coy Mistress"

15. "Dulce et Decorum Est"

16. "Jabberwocky"

17. "The Love Song of J. Alfred Prufrock"

18. "The Red Wheelbarrow"

19. "Stopping by Woods on a Snowy Evening"

20. "Sonnet 130"

26. Inventors And What They Invented - Answer the questions by giving the name of the inventor who invented the named item or items.

1. the phonograph, electric light bulb, and motion picture camera

2. the telephone

3. the Tesla coil and alternating current (AC) electricity

4. the cotton gin

5. the process of pasteurization for preserving food and drinks

6. the lightning rod and bifocal glasses

7. the printing press with moveable type

8. the radio

9. the first successful airplane

10. the Morse code and telegraph

11. the steam engine

12. the first mechanical computer

13. the gasoline-powered automobile

14. the television

15. the World Wide Web

16. co-founded Apple Inc. and helped develop personal computers, smartphones, and other electronics

17. the polio vaccine

18. the first compiler for computer programming languages

19. the Braille writing system for the visually impaired

20. Kevlar, a strong synthetic material used in bulletproof vests and other protective gear.

27. Famous Books And Their Authors - Answer the questions by giving the name of the author who wrote the named book.

1. "To Kill a Mockingbird"

2. "1984"

3. "Pride and Prejudice"

4. "The Catcher in the Rye"

5. "The Great Gatsby"

6. "The Lord of the Rings"

7. "The Chronicles of Narnia"

8. "The Adventures of Huckleberry Finn"

9. "Alice's Adventures in Wonderland"

10. "Brave New World"

11. "Frankenstein"

12. "The Picture of Dorian Gray"

13. "Moby-Dick"

14. "The Scarlet Letter"

15. "The Grapes of Wrath"

16. "One Hundred Years of Solitude"

17. "The Color Purple"

18. "A Tale of Two Cities"

19. "The Adventures of Tom Sawyer"

20. "Anna Karenina"

21. "The Sun Also Rises"

22. "Wuthering Heights"

23. "The Hobbit"

24. "Jane Eyre"

25. "Sense and Sensibility"

26. "The Outsiders"

27. "The Old Man and the Sea"

28. "The Secret Garden"

29. "The Diary of a Young Girl"

30. "The Sound and the Fury"

28. Famous Movies And Their Directors - Answer the questions by giving the name of the director of the movie.

1. The Godfather

2. Pulp Fiction

3. Titanic

4. Jaws

5. The Shawshank Redemption

6. The Silence of the Lambs

7. Star Wars: Episode IV - A New Hope

8. The Wizard of Oz

9. The Lord of the Rings: The Fellowship of the Ring

10. Goodfellas

11. The Matrix

12. Jurassic Park

13. Casablanca

14. The Exorcist

15. Gone with the Wind

16. Psycho

17. E.T. the Extra-Terrestrial

18. A Clockwork Orange

19. Blade Runner

20. The Shining

29. Famous People

1. Who was the first president of the United States?

2. Who was the scientist who formulated the theory of relativity?

3. Who was the British monarch who reigned for more than 63 years and was the longest-reigning monarch in British history until Queen Elizabeth II surpassed her?

4. Who was the author of the "Harry Potter" series of books?

5. Who was the American civil rights activist who famously said, "I have a dream"?

6. Who was the Italian artist and inventor who painted the "Mona Lisa" and "The Last Supper"?

7. Who was the American president who signed the Emancipation Proclamation, which declared slaves in Confederate states to be free?

8. Who was the French military and political leader who rose to prominence during the French Revolution and became the Emperor of France?

9. Who was the American inventor who developed the first commercially successful electric light bulb?

10. Who was the German composer who wrote many of the world's most famous operas, including "The Magic Flute" and "Don Giovanni"?

 30. Famous Quotes And The People Who Said Them - Answer the questions by giving the name of the person who said each memorable quote.

1."The only way to do great work is to love what you do."

2. "In three words I can sum up everything I've learned about life: It goes on."

3. "I have a dream that my four little children will one day live in a nation where they will not be judged by the color of their skin, but by the content of their character."

4. "We can't solve problems by using the same kind of thinking we used when we created them."

5. "The greatest glory in living lies not in never falling, but in rising every time we fall."

6. "Be the change that you wish to see in the world."

7. "I know that I am intelligent, because I know that I know nothing."

8. "I have not failed. I've just found 10,000 ways that won't work."

9. "The only thing we have to fear is fear itself."

10. "All our dreams can come true, if we have the courage to pursue them."

11. "The future belongs to those who believe in the beauty of their dreams."

12. "It does not matter how slowly you go as long as you do not stop."

13. "You miss 100% of the shots you don't take."

14. "Education is the most powerful weapon which you can use to change the world."

"15. The only true wisdom is in knowing you know nothing."

16. "You can't build a reputation on what you are going to do."

17. "Life is 10% what happens to you and 90% how you react to it."

18. "Imagination is more important than knowledge."

19. "The best way to predict the future is to create it."

20. "Success is not final, failure is not fatal: it is the courage to continue that counts."

31. Julius Caesar

1. In what year was Julius Caesar assassinated?

2. In what city was Julius Caesar born?

3. What was Julius Caesar's full name?

4. What position did Julius Caesar hold before becoming dictator of Rome?

5. Who were Julius Caesar's two main allies during the civil war?

6. What famous battle did Julius Caesar win against Pompey in 48 BC?

7. What river did Julius Caesar cross with his army in 49 BC, starting a civil war?

8. Who led the conspiracy to assassinate Julius Caesar?

9. What was the name of Julius Caesar's most famous mistress?

10. Who delivered the famous line, "Et tu, Brute?" during the assassination of Julius Caesar?

11. What was the name of Julius Caesar's nephew and heir?

12. Who wrote the play "Julius Caesar"?

13. What title did Julius Caesar adopt after defeating Cleopatra and Marc Antony?

14. What were the names of Julius Caesar's two wives?

15. What was the name of the Roman festival celebrated on the Ides of March?

16. What famous Roman historian wrote about Julius Caesar?

17. Who was the leader of the Roman Senate at the time of Julius Caesar's assassination?

18. What was the name of Julius Caesar's famous horse?

19. What was Julius Caesar's most famous military campaign?

20. What was the name of the famous Roman general who fought against Julius Caesar in the civil war?

32. William Shakespeare

1. What is the name of Shakespeare's famous tragedy about two star-crossed lovers?

2. In which city was Shakespeare born?

3. Which play by Shakespeare features a character named Hamlet?

4. What is the name of the play that features the character Portia and a famous speech that begins "The quality of mercy is not strained"?

5. What is the name of the play in which the character Prospero gives up his magical powers and forgives his enemies?

6. In which play by Shakespeare is the character Lady Macbeth a central figure?

7. Which play by Shakespeare is set in the city of Verona and features a character named Mercutio?

8. Which Shakespearean play includes the famous line "To be or not to be"?

9. What is the name of the play in which the character Othello is a Moorish general in the Venetian army?

10. Which play by Shakespeare features a group of mechanicals who put on a play-within-a-play?

11. What is the name of the play that features a character named Rosalind who disguises herself as a boy named Ganymede?

12. Which Shakespearean play includes the line "All the world's a stage"?

13. What is the name of the play in which the character Petruchio tries to tame the shrewish Katherine?

14. Which play by Shakespeare is set in the city of Venice and features a character named Iago?

15. What is the name of the play in which the character Caliban is a deformed slave to the magician Prospero?

16. Which play by Shakespeare features the character Malvolio, who is tricked into wearing yellow stockings?

17. What is the name of the play that features the characters Antonio, Bassanio, and Shylock?

18. Which Shakespearean play includes the line "The course of true love never did run smooth"?

19. What is the name of the play in which the character Antony falls in love with Cleopatra?

20. Which play by Shakespeare features the character Falstaff, a friend of the young Prince Hal?

33. Napoleon Bonaparte

1. In what year was Napoleon Bonaparte born?

2. Where was Napoleon Bonaparte born?

3. What was Napoleon's full name?

4. What was Napoleon's height?

5. What was the name of Napoleon's first wife?

6. In what year did Napoleon become the emperor of France?

7. What was the name of Napoleon's most famous battle?

8. Who defeated Napoleon at the Battle of Waterloo?

9. Where was Napoleon exiled after his first defeat?

10. What was the name of Napoleon's second wife?

11. In what year was Napoleon defeated for the final time?

12. Where was Napoleon exiled after his final defeat?

13. What was the name of Napoleon's son?

14. What was the name of Napoleon's brother who also became king of Spain?

15. What was the name of Napoleon's brother who also became king of Naples?

16. Who succeeded Napoleon as the king of France after his exile?

17. In what year was Napoleon's body returned to France from Saint Helena?

18. Where is Napoleon's tomb located?

19. What was Napoleon's famous hat called?

20. What was Napoleon's motto?

34. Abraham Lincoln

1. In what year was Abraham Lincoln assassinated?

2. What was Abraham Lincoln's profession before he became President of the United States?

3. Who was Abraham Lincoln's Vice President?

4. What was the name of the famous speech that Lincoln gave during the Civil War?

5. What was the name of the document that Lincoln issued that declared all slaves in the Confederacy to be free?

6. What was the name of the theater where Lincoln was assassinated?

7. Who was the actor who assassinated Abraham Lincoln?

8. In what year did Lincoln become the 16th President of the United States?

9. What was the name of Lincoln's wife?

10. What was the nickname given to Lincoln's presidency?

11. What was the name of the general who led the Confederate Army during the Civil War?

12. What was the name of the Union general who accepted the surrender of the Confederate Army?

13. What was the name of the legislation that Lincoln signed that allowed settlers to claim land in the West?

14. What was the name of Lincoln's Secretary of State?

15. What was the name of the play that Lincoln was watching when he was assassinated?

16. What was the name of Lincoln's famous speech that began with the words "Four score and seven years ago"?

17. In what year did Lincoln deliver the Emancipation Proclamation?

18. What was the name of the court case that Lincoln argued before the Supreme Court?

19. What was the name of the Union general who was responsible for burning Atlanta during the Civil War?

20. In what year did Lincoln win reelection as President?

35. Theodore Roosevelt

1. What was Theodore Roosevelt's nickname?

2. What was Roosevelt's profession before he became President?

3. What political party did Roosevelt belong to?

4. Which war did Roosevelt serve in?

5. What was the name of the national park system that Roosevelt established?

6. What was Roosevelt's famous slogan?

7. What was Roosevelt's stance on monopolies?

8. What is the name of the famous book Roosevelt wrote about his experiences in the American West?

9. What was the name of Roosevelt's famous charge up San Juan Hill during the Spanish-American War?

10. Which major canal did Roosevelt help build during his presidency?

11. What was Roosevelt's opinion on conservation?

12. What was the name of Roosevelt's famous foreign policy doctrine?

13. What was Roosevelt's policy towards labor unions?

14. What was the name of Roosevelt's famous progressive political platform?

15. What was the name of the famous speech Roosevelt gave after being shot during a presidential campaign?

16. What was Roosevelt's opinion on imperialism?

17. What was Roosevelt's opinion on civil rights?

18. What was Roosevelt's opinion on trusts?

19. What was the name of the famous international peace conference that Roosevelt helped organize?

20. What was the name of Roosevelt's famous environmentalist ally and friend?

36. Nikola Tesla

1. Where was Nikola Tesla born?

2. What was Tesla's education background?

3. What was Tesla's most famous invention?

4. Who was Tesla's main rival in the race to develop electrical systems?

5. What is the Tesla coil used for?

6. What was Tesla's vision for wireless communication?

7. What is the "Tesla effect"?

8. What was Tesla's relationship with J.P. Morgan?

9. What is the Wardenclyffe Tower, and what was Tesla's plan for it?

10. What was the "Tesla turbine"?

11. What was Tesla's view on renewable energy sources?

12. How did Tesla die?

13. What is the "Tesla Roadster"?

14. What was the "Tesla Science Center at Wardenclyffe" project?

15. What was the "War of Currents"?

16. What was Tesla's opinion on Einstein's theory of relativity?

17. What was Tesla's most significant contribution to the field of electrical engineering?

18. What is the "Tesla unit" used for?

19. What is the "Tesla Award"?

20. What was Tesla's opinion on the wireless transmission of power?

37. Ruth Bader Ginsburg

1. What was Ruth Bader Ginsburg's birth name?

2. In which year was Ruth Bader Ginsburg born?

3. In which state was Ruth Bader Ginsburg born?

4. In which year was Ruth Bader Ginsburg appointed to the Supreme Court?

5. Who nominated Ruth Bader Ginsburg to the Supreme Court?

6. What was Ruth Bader Ginsburg's position before being appointed to the Supreme Court?

7. What was Ruth Bader Ginsburg's nickname?

8. What was Ruth Bader Ginsburg's major field of expertise?

9. Which landmark case did Ruth Bader Ginsburg argue before the Supreme Court in 1971?

10. What was Ruth Bader Ginsburg's opinion in the 1973 case Roe v. Wade?

11. Which Supreme Court case did Ruth Bader Ginsburg dissent in, famously wearing a "dissent collar"?

12. Which cancer did Ruth Bader Ginsburg survive multiple times during her lifetime?

13. Which law school did Ruth Bader Ginsburg attend?

14. Which Ivy League university did Ruth Bader Ginsburg receive her undergraduate degree from?

15. Which award did Ruth Bader Ginsburg receive in 2009, which is considered the highest civilian honor in the United States?
16. What was Ruth Bader Ginsburg's stance on the death penalty?

17. Which amendment to the U.S. Constitution did Ruth Bader Ginsburg focus on for much of her career?

18. Which book did Ruth Bader Ginsburg co-write with her former law clerk, Mary Hartnett?

19. Which language did Ruth Bader Ginsburg learn to read at an early age?

20. In which year did Ruth Bader Ginsburg pass away?

38. Queen Elizabeth I

1. Who was Queen Elizabeth I's father?

2. What was Queen Elizabeth I's nickname?

3. What was the name of the queen who preceded Elizabeth I?

4. Who did Elizabeth I defeat in the famous naval battle in 1588?

5. What was the name of the man who tried to assassinate Queen Elizabeth I in 1570?

6. What was the name of Queen Elizabeth I's mother?

7. Who did Elizabeth I consider her greatest enemy?

8. What was the name of the court jester who allegedly made a disrespectful comment about Elizabeth I?

9. Who was the playwright and poet who dedicated his work to Elizabeth I?

10. Who was Elizabeth I's closest advisor and confidant?

11. What was the name of the rebellion that posed a threat to Elizabeth I's reign in 1569?

12. What was the name of the nobleman who Elizabeth I had executed for treason in 1601?

13. Who was the explorer who circumnavigated the globe during Elizabeth I's reign?

14. What was the name of the naval commander who fought alongside Elizabeth I in the battle against the Spanish Armada?

15. Who was Elizabeth I's favorite courtier and rumored lover?

16. What was the name of the queen who succeeded Elizabeth I?

17. What was the name of the man who proposed to Elizabeth I and was subsequently executed for treason?

18. What was the name of the queen who Elizabeth I imprisoned for nearly 20 years?

19. What was the name of the act passed during Elizabeth I's reign that established the Church of England?

20. What was the name of the queen who gave Elizabeth I her nickname, "The Virgin Queen"?

39. Cleopatra

1. What was Cleopatra's ethnicity?

2. Who were Cleopatra's parents?

3. What was Cleopatra's role in ancient Egypt?
Pharaoh of Egypt, ruling from 51 BC until her death in 30 BC.

4. Who were Cleopatra's famous lovers?

5. What was Cleopatra's first language?

6. What was the name of Cleopatra's famous barge?

7. How many children did Cleopatra have?

8. What was the name of Cleopatra's personal physician?

9. How did Cleopatra die?

10. Where is Cleopatra buried?

11. What is the name of the book written about Cleopatra by Stacy Schiff?

12. What is the name of the 1963 movie about Cleopatra, starring Elizabeth Taylor?

13. What was Cleopatra's relationship to her brother Ptolemy XIII?

14. What was the name of Cleopatra's loyal servant and handmaiden?

15. What was Cleopatra's involvement in the Battle of Actium?

16. What did Cleopatra famously wear to her meeting with Mark Antony in Tarsus?

17. What was the name of the Roman general who defeated Cleopatra and Mark Antony?

18. How did Cleopatra gain control of Egypt?

19. How old was Cleopatra when she became ruler of Egypt?

20. What was Cleopatra's full name?

40. Genghis Khan

1. What was the original name of Genghis Khan?

2. What year did Genghis Khan establish the Mongol Empire?

3. What was the name of the first wife of Genghis Khan?

4. What was the name of the city that Genghis Khan captured and destroyed, killing most of its population?

5. What was the name of the Chinese dynasty that was defeated by Genghis Khan's Mongol army?

6. What was the name of Genghis Khan's second son and successor?

7. What was the name of the Persian astronomer and scholar who worked for Genghis Khan?

8. What was the name of the capital city of the Mongol Empire under Genghis Khan's rule?

9. How many campaigns did Genghis Khan lead against the Khwarezmian Empire?

10. What was the name of the Muslim leader who was defeated by Genghis Khan in the Battle of Indus?

11. What was the name of the Chinese general who led the defense against Genghis Khan's invasion of the Jin Dynasty?

12. What was the name of the Muslim city that Genghis Khan's army captured after a long siege?

13. What was the name of the man who was appointed as the first governor of Persia by Genghis Khan?

14. What was the name of the man who succeeded Genghis Khan as the Great Khan of the Mongol Empire?

15. What was the name of the book that Genghis Khan used as a guide for military strategy?

16. What was the name of the Chinese general who surrendered to Genghis Khan and later became his ally?

17. What was the name of the Turkish sultan who defeated Genghis Khan's army in the Battle of Köse Dag?

18. What was the name of the group of warriors who were the elite of Genghis Khan's army?

19. What was the name of the Russian city that was conquered by Genghis Khan's army?

20. What was the name of the Mongol general who led the campaign against the Khwarezmian Empire after Genghis Khan's death?

41. Che Guevara

1. What was Che Guevara's full name?

2. In which country was Che Guevara born?

3. Which famous revolutionary leader did Che Guevara meet in Mexico in 1955?

4. In which country did Che Guevara play a key role in leading a successful revolution in 1959?

5. What was Che Guevara's official position in the Cuban government?

6. Which country did Che Guevara travel to in 1965 to lead a guerrilla warfare campaign?

7. How did Che Guevara die?

8. What is the name of Che Guevara's famous memoir, which was later turned into a movie?

9. In which city is the famous Che Guevara mural located?

10. What is the name of the iconic photo of Che Guevara taken by Alberto Korda?

11. What is the meaning of the famous quote often attributed to Che Guevara, "Hasta la victoria siempre"?

12. Which country has a portrait of Che Guevara on its currency?

13. What is the name of the biography of Che Guevara written by Jon Lee Anderson?

14. What was the title of the speech given by Che Guevara at the United Nations in 1964?

15. Which famous poem did Che Guevara often recite, and is sometimes referred to as "Che's Poem"?

16. What was the name of the group of Argentine revolutionaries that Che Guevara joined in the 1950s?

17. In what year was the iconic image of Che Guevara first used as a symbol of protest?

18. What is the name of the town in Bolivia where Che Guevara was captured and later executed?

19. Which film director made a biographical movie about Che Guevara in 2008?

20. Which other famous revolutionary leader did Che Guevara admire and seek to emulate?

42. Confucius

1. Who was Confucius?

2. What was Confucius' real name?

3. What was the philosophy of Confucius called?

4. What was the name of Confucius' most famous book?

5. What is the central idea of Confucianism?

6. What are the five key relationships in Confucianism?

7. What was the role of education in Confucianism?

8. What was the attitude of Confucianism towards government and politics?

9. What was the attitude of Confucianism towards women?

10. Where did Confucius live most of his life?

11. What is the meaning of the term "Junzi" in Confucianism?

12. What is the Confucian ideal of the "gentleman"?

13. What was the attitude of Confucianism towards war and violence?

14. What was the role of ritual in Confucianism?

15. What was the attitude of Confucianism towards religious belief?

16. What was the attitude of Confucianism towards the family?

17. What was the attitude of Confucianism towards social class?

18. What was the attitude of Confucianism towards knowledge?

19. What was the attitude of Confucianism towards the arts?

20. What is the legacy of Confucianism in Chinese society?

43. Winston Churchill

1. What was the full name of Winston Churchill?

2. What position did Churchill hold when he became Prime Minister of Britain in 1940?

3. Which war was Churchill most famous for leading Britain through?

4. Churchill was born in which city?

5. What did Churchill famously say in a speech during World War II, referring to Britain's refusal to surrender to the Nazis?

6. Churchill was awarded the Nobel Prize in Literature in what year?

7. What political party did Churchill represent during his career?

8. Which famous American leader did Churchill develop a close friendship with during World War II?

9. What was Churchill's famous phrase for the Soviet Union's influence over Eastern Europe after World War II?

10. Churchill served as Prime Minister of Britain for how many non-consecutive terms?

11. Churchill is known for his love of which alcoholic beverage?

12. Churchill's father, Lord Randolph Churchill, held what political position?

13. What was Churchill's main occupation before entering politics?

14. Churchill is credited with coining which term to describe the political alliance between the US and UK during World War II?

15. Churchill was born into which aristocratic family?

16. What was the name of Churchill's wife?

17. Churchill served as a war correspondent during which war before entering politics?

18. Churchill suffered from what medical condition throughout his life?

19. Churchill was a prolific writer, and published over how many books in his lifetime?

20. Churchill's famous "V for Victory" sign was created using which two fingers?

44. Alexander The Great

1. In what year was Alexander the Great born?

2. Who was Alexander's father, the King of Macedon?

3. At what age did Alexander become king?

20. What was the significance of Joan of Arc's victory at Orleans?

The Natural World

46. Animals

1. What is the smallest mammal in the world?

2. What is the tallest animal in the world?

3. What is the only bird that can fly backward?

4. What is the largest animal in the world?

5. What is the largest bird in the world?

6. What is the fastest land animal in the world?

7. What is the slowest mammal in the world?

8. What animal can change its color to blend in with its surroundings?

9. What is the largest reptile in the world?

10. What is the smallest bird in the world?

11. What animal has the longest lifespan?

12. What is the only mammal that can truly fly?

13. What is the largest mammal on land?

14. What is the largest fish in the world?

15. What is the only marsupial native to North America?

16. What is the fastest aquatic animal in the world?

17. What animal can climb trees and hang upside down?

18. What is the largest rodent in the world?

19. What animal is known for its black and white stripes?

20. What is the only species of bear native to South America?

47. Insects

1. Which insect is known for its bright bioluminescence?

2. What is the smallest insect in the world?

3. What insect is known for its ability to roll itself into a ball as a defense mechanism?

4. Which type of insect is the only one capable of making honey?

5. What is the scientific name for the praying mantis?

6. Which insect can carry up to 50 times its body weight?

7. What is the only insect that migrates annually across North America?

8. What is the lifespan of a worker bee?

9. What insect is known for its brightly colored wings and its habit of covering itself in a poisonous foam when threatened?

10. What is the name of the insect that feeds on the blood of mammals, including humans?

11. Which type of insect is known for its ability to change color to blend in with its surroundings?

12. What is the most common type of bee found in North America?

13. What insect is known for its distinctive clicking sound, which is used to attract mates?

14. What is the scientific name for the cockroach?

15. Which insect is capable of jumping up to 30 times its own body length?

16. What is the name of the insect that produces silk and spins webs?

17. What is the largest species of moth in the world?

18. Which insect is known for its highly developed eyesight and is capable of flying at speeds of up to 60 miles per hour?

19. What is the name of the insect that feeds on the blood of other insects?

20. What is the name of the insect that produces the highest-pitched sound in the animal kingdom?

48. Dogs

1. What is the most popular breed of dog in the United States?

2. What breed of dog is the smallest of all breeds?

3. What breed of dog is known as the "gentle giant"?

4. What breed of dog is often used as a guide dog for the blind?

5. What breed of dog is known for its wrinkly skin and droopy face?

6. What breed of dog is known for its blue tongue?

7. What breed of dog is the fastest on Earth?

8. What is the most popular dog name in the United States?

9. What breed of dog is the official dog of Scotland?

10. What breed of dog was originally bred to hunt badgers?

11. What breed of dog is known for its curly coat?

12. What breed of dog is often used in search and rescue operations?

13. What is the only breed of dog that is native to Cuba?

14. What breed of dog is the national dog of Japan?

15. What breed of dog is often associated with fire departments?

16. What breed of dog is known for its short, flat nose?

17. What is the smallest breed of dog in the world?

18. What breed of dog is often used by police forces?

19. What breed of dog was the first animal to orbit Earth?

20. What breed of dog is the most expensive in the world?

49. Cats

1. What is the scientific name for a domestic cat?

2. How many toes does a cat have on each front paw?

3. Which breed of cat is known for its lack of a tail?

4. What is a group of cats called?

5. What is a cat's most highly developed sense?

6. How long is the gestation period for a cat?

7. What is the name of the cat in the movie "Puss in Boots"?

8. What is the name of the cat in "Alice in Wonderland"?

9. What is the name of the cat in the cartoon "Garfield"?

10. Which cat breed is famous for having long, fluffy fur?

11. What is the name of the musical based on T.S. Eliot's "Old Possum's Book of Practical Cats"?

12. What is the name of the cat in the children's book "The Cat in the Hat"?

13. What is the name of the cat in the animated film "The Aristocats"?

14. Which famous scientist had a cat named Schrödinger?

15. What is the name of the cat in the Japanese animated film "My Neighbor Totoro"?

16. What is the name of the cat in the musical "Cats" who is known for his magic abilities?

17. Which cat breed is known for its blue eyes and pointed coat pattern?

18. What is the name of the cat in the book series "Warriors"?

19. What is the name of the cat in the animated series "Tom and Jerry"?

20. What is the name of the cat in the comic strip "Garfield" who is known for his love of lasagna?

50. Elephants

1. What is the largest land animal on Earth?

2. What is the average weight of a male elephant?

3. What is the average weight of a female elephant?

4. How many teeth do elephants have?

5. What is the lifespan of an elephant?

6. What is the gestation period for an elephant?

7. What is the name for a group of elephants?

8. What is the name for a male elephant?

9. What is the name for a female elephant?

10. What is the name for a baby elephant?

11. What is the scientific name for an elephant?

12. How many species of elephants are there?

13. What is the difference between African and Asian elephants?

14. How much do elephants eat in a day?

15. What is an elephant's favorite food?

16. How many muscles are in an elephant's trunk?

17. How fast can an elephant run?

18. Can elephants swim?

19. How do elephants communicate with each other?

20. Are elephants endangered?

51. Turtles

1. What is the scientific name for a turtle?

2. How many species of turtles are there?

3. What is the largest species of turtle in the world?

4. What is the smallest species of turtle in the world?

5. Do turtles have teeth?

6. How long can turtles hold their breath?

7. How do turtles protect themselves from predators?

8. What is the oldest recorded age of a turtle?

9. What is the difference between a turtle and a tortoise?

10. What is the name of the famous teenage mutant ninja turtle who wears a blue mask?

11. Which species of turtle is known for its long neck?

12. What is the name of the world's largest freshwater turtle?

13. How do turtles lay eggs?

14. What do turtles eat?

15. What is the name of the famous children's book about a turtle?

16. Can turtles swim upside down?

17. What is the name of the famous animated character who is a turtle?

18. What is the name of the critically endangered sea turtle species that is native to Mexico?

19. Do turtles have ears?

20. How fast can turtles run?

52. Fish

1. What type of fish is the primary ingredient in traditional fish and chips?

2. Which type of fish is also known as a "swimming liver"?

3. What type of fish is the primary ingredient in sushi rolls?

4. What is the name of the famous animated clownfish who lives in the Pacific Ocean?

5. What type of fish is also known as a "toothy predator" and is commonly found in freshwater?

6. What is the most popular fish in the United States by consumption?

7. What type of fish is also known as "silver salmon" and is commonly found in the Pacific Ocean?

8. What type of fish is a popular seafood delicacy in Japan and is known for its unique texture?

9. What type of fish is also known as a "mudfish" and can breathe air out of water?

10. What type of fish is the primary ingredient in the popular British dish, kedgeree?

11. What type of fish is known for its bright orange eggs, often served in sushi rolls?

12. What type of fish is known for its flat body and ability to camouflage itself in sandy ocean floors?

13. What type of fish is also known as a "horned fish" and is known for its sharp spines?

14. What type of fish is commonly found in British waters and is often used in fish pies?

15. What type of fish is also known as a "king of the sea" and is commonly found in the Mediterranean?

16. What type of fish is known for its sharp teeth and ability to swim upstream to spawn?

17. What type of fish is a popular seafood delicacy in France and is known for its buttery texture?

18. What type of fish is known for its flat, circular shape and is often used in sushi rolls?

19. What type of fish is commonly found in North America and is known for its bright red flesh?

20. What type of fish is also known as a "parrotfish" and is known for its brightly colored scales?

53. Sharks

1. How many species of sharks are there in the world?

2. Which species of shark is the largest?

3. What is the fastest species of shark?

4. What is the smallest species of shark?

5. Which species of shark is known for its distinctive hammer-shaped head?

6. What is the largest predatory fish in the ocean?

7. What type of shark is also known as the "sea tiger"?

8. What type of shark is known for its long, pointed snout and serrated teeth?

9. What is the most dangerous species of shark to humans?

10. What type of shark is known for jumping out of the water?

11. What is the largest shark ever recorded?

12. What type of shark is known for its unique pattern of spots?

13. What type of shark is known for living in freshwater?

14. What type of shark is known for its distinctive black tip on its fins?

15. What type of shark is known for its flattened body and ability to camouflage itself on the ocean floor?
15. The angel shark is known for its flattened body and ability to camouflage itself on the ocean floor.
16. What type of shark is known for its long, narrow body and ability to swim at high speeds?

17. What type of shark is known for its ability to produce a glowing blue-green light?

18. What type of shark is known for its prehistoric appearance?

19. What type of shark is known for its saw-like snout and ability to sense electrical fields?

20. What type of shark is known for its long, slender body and ability to swim great distances?

54. Dinosaurs

1. What is the largest known dinosaur ever discovered?

2. What is the name of the smallest known dinosaur?

3. What is the name of the dinosaur that had a skull that was over 6 feet long?

4. What is the name of the dinosaur that had three horns on its face?

5. What is the name of the dinosaur that had a long neck and tail and was over 70 feet long?

6. What is the name of the dinosaur that was covered in feathers?

7. What is the name of the dinosaur that could fly?

8. What is the name of the dinosaur that had a club-like tail?

9. What is the name of the dinosaur that was discovered in Antarctica?

10. What is the name of the dinosaur that had a brain the size of a walnut?

11. What is the name of the dinosaur that had a bony frill around its neck?

12. What is the name of the dinosaur that had a mouth full of razor-sharp teeth and was over 30 feet long?

13. What is the name of the dinosaur that had a sail on its back?

14. What is the name of the dinosaur that had the longest arms in relation to its body size?

15. What is the name of the dinosaur that had a horn on its nose?

16. What is the name of the dinosaur that was the largest predator to ever walk the Earth?

17. What is the name of the dinosaur that had a long, thin snout and was named after a famous paleontologist?

18. What is the name of the dinosaur that was believed to have lived in groups and traveled in herds?

19. What is the name of the dinosaur that had a long, curved neck and was the tallest dinosaur ever discovered?

55. Phobias - Answer the questions by giving the name of the phobia that matches the given definition.

1. Fear of spiders.

8. What is the average distance between Jupiter and the Sun?

9. What is the surface temperature of Jupiter?

10. What is the size of Jupiter compared to Earth?

11. What is the atmosphere of Jupiter mainly composed of?

12. What is the name of the largest moon of Jupiter?

13. What is the name of the second-largest moon of Jupiter?

14. What is the name of the third-largest moon of Jupiter?

15. What is the name of the fourth-largest moon of Jupiter?

16. What is the name of the spacecraft that discovered the four largest moons of Jupiter?

17. What is the name of the mission that explored Jupiter and its moons in the 1990s?

18. What is the name of the spacecraft that discovered water vapor plumes on Jupiter's moon Europa?

19. What is the name of the mission that will explore Jupiter's moon Europa in the 2020s?

20. What is the name of the asteroid that is believed to be a captured moon of Jupiter?

58. Space

1. What is the name of our galaxy?

2. What is the distance from Earth to the Sun?

3. What is the largest planet in the Solar System?

4. What is the name of the first man to walk on the moon?

5. What is the name of the first artificial satellite to be launched into space?
6. What is the name of the first American woman to walk in space?

7. What is the name of the spacecraft that took the first image of Earth from space?

8. What is the name of the telescope that was launched in 1990 and is still in operation?

9. What is the name of the spacecraft that was launched in 1977 and has now left the Solar System?

10. What is the name of the spacecraft that has been studying Saturn and its moons since 2004?

11. What is the name of the mission that is currently studying Mars?

12. What is the name of the phenomenon that causes the Northern Lights?

13. What is the name of the phenomenon that causes the Southern Lights?

14. What is the name of the first commercial spacecraft to take astronauts to the International Space Station?

15. What is the name of the first privately-funded mission to the Moon?

16. What is the name of the largest asteroid in the Solar System?

17. What is the name of the brightest star in the night sky?

18. What is the name of the constellation that contains the North Star?

19. What is the name of the spacecraft that was sent to explore Pluto and the Kuiper Belt?

20. What is the name of the mission that will send the first woman and next man to the Moon?

59. The Universe

1. What is the estimated age of the universe?

2. What is the name of the theory that explains the beginning of the universe?

3. What is the name of the force that is responsible for the expansion of the universe?

4. What is the name of the largest structure in the universe?

5. What is the name of the supermassive black hole at the center of our galaxy?

6. What is the name of the largest known star in the universe?

7. What is the name of the first exoplanet to be discovered?

8. What is the name of the theory that suggests there are multiple universes?

9. What is the name of the process that powers the sun?

10. What is the name of the closest galaxy to the Milky Way?

11. What is the name of the spacecraft that is currently traveling to the edge of the Solar System?

12. What is the name of the phenomenon that occurs when a massive star explodes?

13. What is the name of the force that holds the universe together?

14. What is the name of the galaxy that is home to the nearest quasar?

15. What is the name of the space telescope that is used to study the universe?

16. What is the name of the phenomenon that occurs when a star collapses into a single point?

17. What is the name of the space mission that discovered thousands of exoplanets?

18. What is the name of the constellation that contains the stars that form the Big Dipper?

19. What is the name of the galaxy that contains the largest known black hole?

20. What is the name of the mission that is currently studying the composition and history of the universe?

Sports

60. Famous Athletes

1. Who is the fastest man in the world with a record of 9.58 seconds in 100m?

2. Who is the only NBA player to win MVP, Finals MVP, and All-Star Game MVP awards in the same season?

3. Who is the all-time leading scorer in NBA history?

4. Which famous golfer has won 18 major championships during his career?

5. Who is the most decorated Olympian of all time with 28 medals?

6. Who is the only male tennis player to win a calendar-year Grand Slam?

7. Who is the first and only female gymnast to win three all-around titles at the Olympics?

8. Who holds the record for most goals scored in a single season in Europe's top five leagues?

9. Who is the only NFL player to win five Super Bowl championships as a starting quarterback?

10. Who is the first African-American woman to win an individual Olympic gold medal in gymnastics?

11. Who is the first player in NBA history to win MVP, Defensive Player of the Year, and NBA Finals MVP awards in the same season?

12. Who is the first and only woman to win the Grand Slam in tennis twice?

13. Who is the first boxer to win titles in eight different weight classes?

14. Who is the only soccer player to win three World Cups?

15. Who is the first African-American woman to win a Grand Slam singles title?

16. Who is the youngest player to score a hat-trick in the English Premier League?

17. Who is the only basketball player to win an NCAA championship, an NBA championship, and an Olympic gold medal in the same year?

18. Who is the first and only woman to complete a triple axel in the Olympics?

19. Who is the all-time leading scorer for the United States women's national soccer team?

20. Who is the first NBA player to have 30,000 points, 6,000 rebounds, and 6,000 assists in a career?

61. Soccer/Football

1. Which country won the 2018 FIFA World Cup?

2. Who is the all-time leading scorer in the English Premier League?

3. Which two teams have won the most Super Bowls in NFL history?

4. Which country won the first ever FIFA World Cup in 1930?

5. Who won the Ballon d'Or award in 2020?

6. Who holds the record for the most goals scored in a single season of the English Premier League?

7. Which team won the UEFA Champions League in 2021?

8. Who is the only player to have won the Ballon d'Or while playing for a team outside of Europe?

9. Who is the all-time leading scorer for the Brazilian national team?

10. Which country won the first ever UEFA European Football Championship in 1960?

11. Which team has won the most UEFA Champions League titles in history?

12. Who is the only player to have won the FIFA World Cup, UEFA Champions League, and Ballon d'Or in the same year?

13. Which country has won the most Copa America titles in history?

14. Who is the all-time leading scorer in the history of the Spanish La Liga?

15. Which team won the Premier League title in the 2020-2021 season?

16. Who won the FIFA Women's World Cup in 2019?

17. Which player has won the most Ballon d'Or awards in history?

18. Which team won the European Championship in 2016?

19. Who is the all-time leading scorer in the history of the Italian Serie A?

20. Which country has won the most FIFA World Cup titles in history?

62. NFL

1. What is the oldest team in the NFL?

2. Which team has won the most Super Bowl championships?

3. Who holds the record for the most career touchdown passes in NFL history?

4. Which team holds the record for the longest winning streak in NFL history?

5. Who is the all-time leading rusher in NFL history?

6. Which NFL team has the most players in the Pro Football Hall of Fame?

7. Who is the only player to have won five Super Bowl MVP awards?

8. Which team won the first ever Super Bowl in 1967?

9. Which NFL team is nicknamed the "Steel Curtain"?

10. Who is the only player to have won the NFL MVP award five times?

11. Which team won the Super Bowl in 2021?

12. Who holds the record for the most career receiving yards in NFL history?

13. Which team has won the most NFL championships (pre-Super Bowl era)?

14. Who is the only player to have rushed for 2,000 yards in a single NFL season?

15. Which team is the only one to have gone undefeated throughout an entire NFL season, including playoffs?

10. Who was the first African American to play in Major League Baseball?

11. Who holds the record for the most career hits in a single Major League Baseball team?

12. What is the only team to have played in four different cities?

13. Who is the only player to have won the Cy Young Award unanimously twice?

14. Who holds the record for the most home runs hit in a single month?

15. Who is the only player to have won the World Series MVP award on a losing team?

16. Which pitcher holds the record for the most no-hitters in Major League Baseball history?

17. Which team has won the most World Series championships?

18. Who is the only player to have won the American League Rookie of the Year award unanimously?

19. Who holds the record for the most stolen bases in a single season?

20. Which pitcher holds the record for the lowest career earned run average in Major League Baseball history?

65. NFL Teams And The Cities and States They Are From - Answer the questions by giving the name of the city and state that is the the location of the team's home field.

1. Arizona Cardinals
2. Atlanta Falcons
3. Baltimore Raven
4. Buffalo Bills
5. Carolina Panthers
6. Chicago Bears
7. Cincinnati Bengals
8. Cleveland Browns
9. Dallas Cowboys
10. Denver Broncos
11. Detroit Lions
12. Green Bay Packers

13. Houston Texans
14. Indianapolis Colts
15. Jacksonville Jaguars
16. Kansas City Chiefs
17. Las Vegas Raiders
18. Los Angeles Chargers
19. Los Angeles Rams
20. Miami Dolphins
21. Minnesota Vikings
22. New England Patriots
23. New Orleans Saints
24. New York Giants
25. New York Jets
26. Philadelphia Eagles
27. Pittsburgh Steelers
28. San Francisco 49ers
29. Seattle Seahawks
30. Tampa Bay Buccaneers
31. Tennessee Titans
32. Washington Football Team

Geography

66. Geography

1. What is the tallest structure in Paris?

2. What is the largest pyramid in Egypt?

3. What is the name of the famous palace in India, which is now a UNESCO World Heritage site?

4. What is the name of the famous prehistoric monument in England?

5. What is the name of the famous street in New York City that is known for its bright lights and billboards?

6. What is the name of the famous amusement park in California?

7. What is the name of the famous bridge in San Francisco, California?

8. What is the name of the famous waterfall on the border of Canada and the United States?

9. What is the name of the famous church in Vatican City?

10. What is the name of the famous palace in Moscow that is now a museum?

11. What is the name of the famous theme park in Orlando, Florida?

12. What is the name of the famous canyon located in Arizona?

13. What is the name of the famous opera house in Australia?

14. What is the name of the famous tower in London that houses the Crown Jewels?

15. What is the name of the famous fountain located in Rome, Italy?

16. What is the name of the famous museum in Paris that houses the Mona Lisa?

17. What is the name of the famous palace in Versailles, France?

18. What is the name of the famous monument located in Washington, D.C.?

19. What is the name of the famous hotel in Dubai that is shaped like a sail?

20. What is the name of the famous stadium in Rio de Janeiro, Brazil?

67. National Parks In The United States With Their Respective States - Answer the questions by giving the name of the US state where the given national park is located.

1. Acadia National Park
2. Arches National Park
3. Badlands National Park
4. Big Bend National Park
5. Bryce Canyon National Park
6. Canyonlands National Park
7. Capitol Reef National Park
8.. Channel Islands National Park
9. Crater Lake National Park
10. Death Valley National Park

11. Denali National Park
12. Everglades National Park
13. Glacier Bay National Park
14. Glacier National Park
15. Grand Canyon National Park
16. Grand Teton National Park
17. Great Smoky Mountains National Park
18. Joshua Tree National Park
19. Kenai Fjords National Park
20. Kings Canyon National Park
21. Lassen Volcanic National Park
22. Olympic National Park
23. Petrified Forest National Park
24. Redwood National and State Parks
25. Rocky Mountain National Park
26. Sequoia National Park
27. Yellowstone National Park
28. Yosemite National Park
29. Zion National Park
30. Voyageurs National Park

68. Countries And Their Leaders - Answer the questions by giving the name of the country that the given person leads or has led.

1. President Joe Biden
2. Prime Minister Boris Johnson
3. President Emmanuel Macron
4. Chancellor Angela Merkel
5. President Vladimir Putin
6. President Xi Jinping
7. Prime Minister Yoshihide Suga
8. President Moon Jae-in
9. President Jair Bolsonaro
10. President Andrés Manuel López Obrador
11. Prime Minister Justin Trudeau
12. Prime Minister Narendra Modi
13. Prime Minister Imran Khan
14. Prime Minister Scott Morrison
15. Prime Minister Jacinda Ardern
16. President Cyril Ramaphosa

17. President Muhammadu Buhari
18. King Salman bin Abdulaziz Al Saud
19. Supreme Leader Ali Khamenei and President Ebrahim Raisi
20. Prime Minister Benjamin Netanyahu (as of May 2021)

69. U.S. States And Their Capitals - Answer the questions by giving the name of the city that is the capital of the US state given.

1. Alabama
2. Alaska
3. Arizona
4. Arkansas
5. California
6. Colorado
7. Connecticut
8. Delaware
9. Florida
10. Georgia
11. Hawaii
12. Idaho
13. Illinois
14. Indiana
15. Iowa
16. Kansas
17. Kentucky
18. Louisiana
19. Maine
20. Maryland
21. Massachusetts
22. Michigan
23. Minnesota
24. Mississippi
25. Missouri
26. Montana
27. Nebraska
28. Nevada
29. New Hampshire
30. New Jersey
31. New Mexico
32. New York

33. North Carolina
34. North Dakota
35. Ohio
36. Oklahoma
37.Oregon
38. Pennsylvania
39. Rhode Island
40. South Carolin
41. South Dakota
42. Tennessee
43. Texas
44. Utah
45. Vermont
46. Virginia
47. Washington
48. West Virginia
49. Wisconsin
50. Wyoming

70. Countries With Their Capitals - Answer the questions by giving the name of the city that is the capital of the country given.

1. Afghanistan
2. Argentina
3. Australia
4. Brazil
5. Canada
6. China
7. Denmark
8. Egypt
9. France
10. Germany
11. Greece
12. India
13. Iran
14. Iraq
15. Ireland
16. Israel
17. Italy 1
18. Japan

1. A
2. B
3. B
4. C
5. C
6. E
7. G
8. P
9. P
10. S
11. U
12. V
13. F

Music

73. Musical Instruments

1. What is the name of the smallest member of the violin family?

2. What is the name of the largest member of the violin family?

3. What is the instrument that is also known as a squeezebox?

4. What type of instrument is the kazoo?

5. Which instrument is played by blowing into a pipe and squeezing a bag?

6. What percussion instrument is played by striking two wooden sticks together?

7. What type of instrument is a didgeridoo?

8. What is the name of the brass instrument that is commonly used in jazz music?

9. What is the name of the percussion instrument that is played by shaking it back and forth?

10. Which instrument is played by sliding a metal or glass tube along a set of pipes?

11. What is the name of the stringed instrument that is played with a bow?

12. Which instrument is played by plucking the strings with the fingers?

13. What is the name of the keyboard instrument that produces sound by striking strings with hammers?

14. Which instrument is played by blowing into a mouthpiece and pressing keys to change the pitch?

15. What is the name of the percussion instrument that is made of a wooden box with metal keys?

16. Which instrument is played by blowing air across the top of a hole and pressing keys to change the pitch?

17. What is the name of the percussion instrument that consists of a pair of wooden bars that are struck together?

18. Which instrument is played by plucking the strings with a set of metal tines?

19. What is the name of the percussion instrument that is played by striking a set of metal bars with a hammer?

20. Which instrument is played by blowing into a metal mouthpiece and using valves to change the pitch?

74. 1960s Bands

1. What 1960s band was known for hits such as "Hey Jude" and "Let It Be"?

2. What was the name of the famous 1960s band fronted by Mick Jagger and Keith Richards?

3. Which 1960s band's hits included "Purple Haze" and "Foxy Lady"?

4. What 1960s American rock band had hits with "Good Vibrations" and "Wouldn't It Be Nice"?

5. Who was the lead singer of the 1960s band The Doors?

6. What 1960s band was known for hits such as "Light My Fire" and "Break on Through (To the Other Side)"?

7. Which British band's 1960s hits included "Paint It Black" and "Satisfaction"?

8. What band's 1960s hits included "Born to Be Wild" and "Magic Carpet Ride"?

9. What 1960s band was known for hits such as "All Along the Watchtower" and "The Wind Cries Mary"?

10. What 1960s American rock band's hits included "Proud Mary" and "Bad Moon Rising"?

11. What 1960s band was known for hits such as "California Dreamin'" and "Monday, Monday"?

12. What 1960s band had hits such as "The House of the Rising Sun" and "Don't Let Me Be Misunderstood"?

13. What 1960s American rock band's hits included "I Got You Babe" and "The Beat Goes On"?

14. What 1960s British rock band was known for hits such as "My Generation" and "Pinball Wizard"?

15. What 1960s band's hits included "White Rabbit" and "Somebody to Love"?

16. What band's 1960s hits included "Do You Believe in Magic" and "Summer in the City"?

17. What 1960s British rock band was known for hits such as "Sunshine of Your Love" and "White Room"?

18. What 1960s American rock band's hits included "For What It's Worth" and "Mr. Soul"?

19. What 1960s band's hits included "Aquarius/Let the Sunshine In" and "Up, Up and Away"?

20. What 1960s British rock band's hits included "All Day and All of the Night" and "You Really Got Me"?

75. 1970s Bands

1. Which band's debut album was released in 1971 and included the hits "Stairway to Heaven" and "Black Dog"?

2. What band, formed in 1977, featured Debbie Harry as its lead singer?

3. What American rock band is often associated with the 1970s and had hits like "Sweet Emotion" and "Dream On"?

4. What British band had a hit song in 1975 with "Bohemian Rhapsody"?

5. What band, named after a street in London, released its album "London Calling" in 1979?

6. What band's 1976 album "Hotel California" included the hit songs "Hotel California" and "New Kid in Town"?

7. What American band, fronted by Barry Gibb, had a string of hits in the 1970s including "Stayin' Alive" and "How Deep Is Your Love"?

8. What British band had a hit song in 1972 with "Stairway to Heaven"?

9. What band, whose members included Mick Jagger and Keith Richards, had a hit song in 1971 with "Brown Sugar"?

10. What American band had a hit song in 1976 with "More Than a Feeling"?

11. What British band had a hit song in 1975 with "S.O.S."?

12. What American band had a hit song in 1972 with "Long Cool Woman in a Black Dress"?

13. What Canadian band, formed in 1968, had a hit song in 1970 with "American Woman"?

14. What British band had a hit song in 1979 with "Another Brick in the Wall"?

15. What American band had a hit song in 1973 with "We're an American Band"?

16. What British band had a hit song in 1978 with "Stayin' Alive"?

17. What American band had a hit song in 1979 with "My Sharona"?

18. What British band had a hit song in 1974 with "Killer Queen"?

19. What American band had a hit song in 1974 with "Sweet Home Alabama"?

20. What British singer had a hit song in 1977 with "Heroes"?

76. 1980s Bands

1. What band, fronted by a flamboyant lead singer known for his high-pitched vocals, released the album "1984" in 1984?

2. What band, formed in Liverpool, England, was known for their catchy pop tunes in the early 80s, including "Karma Chameleon" and "Do You Really Want to Hurt Me"?

3. What all-female rock band released the hit song "Love Is a Battlefield" in 1983?

4. What British band, fronted by Robert Smith, had hits in the 80s with songs like "Just Like Heaven" and "Lovecats"?

5. What American heavy metal band, known for their theatrical live performances and hit songs like "Home Sweet Home" and "Dr. Feelgood," formed in the early 80s?

6. What band, known for their signature mullets and hits like "Africa" and "Rosanna," was formed in Los Angeles in 1976?

7. What British rock band, fronted by Freddie Mercury, had hits in the 80s with songs like "Another One Bites the Dust" and "Radio Ga Ga"?

8. What American rock band, fronted by Bruce Springsteen, had hits in the 80s with songs like "Born in the U.S.A." and "Dancing in the Dark"?

9. What band, fronted by Bono, formed in Dublin, Ireland, in 1976 and had hits in the 80s with songs like "Pride (In the Name of Love)" and "With or Without You"?

10. What American new wave band, known for their quirky style and hits like "Whip It" and "Peek-a-Boo," formed in Akron, Ohio, in 1972?

11. What American rock band, known for their blues-influenced sound and hits like "Legs" and "Sharp Dressed Man," formed in Texas in 1969?

12. What British band, fronted by Sting, had hits in the 80s with songs like "Every Breath You Take" and "Message in a Bottle"?

13. What American heavy metal band, known for their outrageous stage antics and hits like "Welcome to the Jungle" and "Sweet Child o' Mine," formed in the early 80s?

14. What American rock band, known for their power ballads and hits like "Sister Christian" and "Don't Tell Me You Love Me," formed in California in 1979?

15. What British band, known for their synthesis of rock and classical music and hits like "Owner of a Lonely Heart," formed in London in 1968?

16. What American rock band, fronted by David Lee Roth, had hits in the 80s with songs like "Jump" and "Panama"?

17. What American new wave band, known for their punk-influenced sound and hits like "Blister in the Sun" and "Add It Up," formed in Milwaukee, Wisconsin, in 1981?

18. What British band, known for their alternative rock sound and hits like "How Soon Is Now?" and "Bigmouth Strikes Again," formed in Manchester in 1982?

77. 1990s Bands

1. Which grunge band's hits include "Black," "Jeremy," and "Even Flow"?

2. What band was led by singer/songwriter Thom Yorke and had hits like "Karma Police" and "Creep"?

3. What Irish band was fronted by Bono and had hits like "With or Without You" and "One"?

4. What alternative rock band's hits include "Smells Like Teen Spirit" and "Come As You Are"?

5. Which band, fronted by Billie Joe Armstrong, had hits like "When I Come Around" and "Basket Case"?

6. What band was fronted by Kurt Cobain and had hits like "Lithium" and "All Apologies"?

7. What all-female band's hits include "Waterfalls" and "No Scrubs"?

8. What English rock band was led by singer Robert Smith and had hits like "Friday I'm In Love" and "Just Like Heaven"?

9. What band was led by singer Eddie Vedder and had hits like "Better Man" and "Alive"?

10. What American rock band's hits include "Black Hole Sun" and "Spoonman"?

5. What is the main ingredient in guacamole?

6. What type of cheese is used in a traditional Caesar salad?

7. What is the main ingredient in risotto?

8. What is the most popular spice in the world?

9. What type of meat is traditionally used in a Swedish meatball?

10. What is the national dish of Spain?

11. Which type of cuisine does the dish 'Sushi' belong to?

12. What is the national dish of Italy?

13. Which fruit is known as the 'king of fruits' in Southeast Asia?

14. What type of cuisine does the dish 'Tandoori Chicken' belong to?

15. What is the main ingredient in the Middle Eastern dip 'Baba Ghanoush'?

16. What is the main ingredient in the dish 'Huevos Rancheros'?

17. What is the national dish of Thailand?

18. What type of bread is used in a traditional French croque-monsieur sandwich?

19. What is the main ingredient in the Mexican dip 'Queso'?

20. Which type of nut is used in the traditional pesto sauce recipe?

80. Desserts

1. What dessert is traditionally made with ladyfingers, mascarpone cheese, and coffee?

2. What type of pastry is used to make profiteroles?

3. What is the main ingredient in the Italian dessert cannoli?

4. What popular dessert is made from mixing whipped egg whites and sugar?

5. What is the national dessert of England?

6. What is the primary ingredient in the Middle Eastern dessert baklava?

7. What is the French word for the classic dessert known as "burnt cream"?

8. What type of fruit is traditionally used to make a tarte tatin?

9. What is the main ingredient in the Italian dessert panna cotta?

10. What is the name of the traditional Mexican dessert made from fried dough covered in cinnamon sugar?

11. What type of pie is named after a citrus fruit?

12. What type of cake is traditionally served during the holiday season in the United States?

13. What dessert is made by layering ice cream and cake, and then covering the entire thing in whipped cream?

14. What popular dessert is made from baking a mixture of flour, sugar, butter, and eggs?

15. What is the name of the Italian dessert that translates to "pick me up"?

16. What is the name of the classic French dessert made from layers of puff pastry and pastry cream?

17. What is the name of the American dessert made from baked apples and a crumbly topping of flour, sugar, and butter?

18. What is the name of the traditional Indian dessert made from milk, sugar, and saffron?

19. What is the name of the Greek dessert made from phyllo dough and honey syrup?

20. What is the name of the Mexican dessert made from a sweetened condensed milk caramel?

81. Beers And Where They're From - Answer the questions by giving the name of the country that each beer is originally from.

1. Guinness
2. Heineken
3. Corona
4. Stella Artois
5. Budweiser
6. Beck's
7. Tsingtao
8. Asahi
9. Carlsberg
10. Efes Pilsen
11. Singha
12. Peroni
13. Kronenbourg 1664
14. San Miguel
15. Victoria Bitter (VB)
16. Dos Equis
17. Harp
18. Tiger Beer
19. Sapporo
20. Mythos
21. Chang Beer
22. Polar
23. Cusqueña
24. Baltika
25. La Trappe
26. Chimay
27. Fuller's London Pride
28. Negra Modelo
29. Red Stripe
30. Moosehead

82. Alcoholic Spirits and Where They're From - Answer the questions by giving the name of the country that each alcoholic spirit is originally from.

1. Tequila
2. Vodka
3. Rum
4. Scotch whisky
5. Bourbon whiskey

6. Irish whiskey
7. Cognac
8. Gin
9. Sake
10. Pisco
11. Calvados
12. Grappa
13. Soju
14. Baijiu
15. Shochu
16. Armagnac
17. Rakia
18. Slivovitz
19. Aquavit
20. Mezcal
21. Absinthe
22. Ouzo
23. Raki
24. Akvavit
25. Pálinka
26. Damson gin
27. Jenever
28. Aguardiente
29. Fernet
30. Amaro

83. Drinks And Their Ingredients - Answer the questions by giving the name of the drink that is made with the given ingredients.

1. tequila, triple sec, lime juice
2. gin or vodka, dry vermouth
3. bourbon or rye whiskey, sugar, bitters, orange peel
4. bourbon or rye whiskey, sweet vermouth, bitters, cherry
5. rum, lime juice, simple syrup
6. vodka, ginger beer, lime juice
7. rum, lime juice, simple syrup, mint leaves, club soda
8. vodka, tomato juice, Worcestershire sauce, hot sauce, lemon juice, celery salt, pepper
9. gin, sweet vermouth, Campari
10. vodka, triple sec, cranberry juice, lime juice
11. vodka, gin, rum, tequila, triple sec, sour mix, cola

12. rum, lime juice, orange curaçao, orgeat syrup
13. cognac or brandy, triple sec, lemon juice
14. gin, tonic water, lime wedge
15. bourbon or rye whiskey, lemon juice, simple syrup
16. rum, pineapple juice, coconut cream
17. vodka, coffee liqueur, cream
18. tequila, orange juice, grenadine
19. gin, cherry brandy, triple sec, pineapple juice, lime juice, grenadine, Angostura bitters
20. dark rum, ginger beer, lime juice

84. Dishes And Where They're From - Answer the questions by giving the name of the country that each dish is originally from.

1. Paella
2. Sushi
3. Moussaka
4. Pad Thai
5. Peking duck
6. Tacos
7. Carbonara
8. Wiener schnitzel
9. Borscht
10. Fish and chips
11. Coq au vin
12. Kimchi
13. Goulash
14. Rendang
15. Chicken tikka masala
16. Poutine
17. Feijoada
18. Kebab
19. Smörgåsbord
20. Ceviche
21. Sushi
22. Tacos
23. Bangers and mash
24. Kebab
25. Pad Thai
26. Sauerkraut
27. Pizza

Miscellaneous

Gods

85. Greek Gods And Their abilities - Answer the questions by giving the name of the Greek god that has the mentioned abilities.

1. god of thunder and lightning, king of the gods
2. god of the sea, earthquakes, and horses
3. god of the underworld and the dead
5. goddess of marriage, childbirth, and family
5. goddess of wisdom, war, and crafts
6. god of music, poetry, prophecy, and archery
7. goddess of the hunt, childbirth, and the moon
8. god of war and violence
9. goddess of love and beauty
10. goddess of agriculture and fertility
11. god of commerce, thieves, travelers, and messages
12. god of fire, metalworking, and blacksmiths
13. god of wine, parties, and ecstasy
14. goddess of the hearth, home, and family
15. queen of the underworld, goddess of spring and vegetation
16. god of love and desire
17. god of the sun
18. goddess of the moon
19. god of dreams
20. goddess of retribution and revenge.

86. Roman gods And Their Abilities - Answer the questions by giving the name of the Roman god that has the mentioned abilities.

1. king of the gods, god of thunder and lightning, and protector of the state
2. queen of the gods, goddess of marriage, and protector of women
3. god of the sea, earthquakes, and horses
4. god of the underworld and the dead
5. goddess of love and beauty
6. god of war and agriculture
7. god of commerce, thieves, travelers, and messenger of the gods
8. god of music, poetry, prophecy, and the sun

9. goddess of the hunt, wild animals, and childbirth
10. god of wine, ecstasy, and theater
11. goddess of agriculture and the harvest
12. goddess of the hearth and home
13. god of beginnings and endings, gates, doors, and transitions
14. god of nature, forests, and fertility
15. goddess of wisdom, war, and crafts
16. goddess of springtime, flowers, and fertility
17. god of agriculture, time, and the harvest
18. god of fire, blacksmiths, and volcanoes
19. god of love and desire
20. goddess of luck and fate.

87. Egyptian Gods And Their Abilities - Answer the questions by giving the name of the Egyptian god that has the mentioned abilities.

1. god of the sun and creation, associated with falcons and the pharaohs
2. god of the afterlife, associated with the Nile River and fertility
3. goddess of motherhood and fertility, associated with the throne and the pharaohs
4. god of the sky, associated with the pharaohs and falcons
5. god of embalming and mummification, associated with jackals and funerary rites
6. god of writing, wisdom, and the moon, associated with baboons and ibises
7. goddess of love, music, and dance, associated with cows and the sky
8. goddess of war and destruction, associated with lions and the sun
9. god of chaos and storms, associated with donkeys and the desert
10. goddess of cats, protection, and joy, associated with domestic cats and the home

Other

88. Cars

1. Which Italian sports car manufacturer is known for their prancing horse logo?

2. What does the acronym BMW stand for?

3. What is the top speed of a Bugatti Veyron?

4. Which automaker produces the Mustang?

5. What car company makes the Camry?

6. What does the acronym AMG stand for in Mercedes-AMG?

7. Which automaker produces the Corvette?

8. What is the fastest production car in the world as of 2021?

9. What does the acronym SUV stand for?

10. Which German car manufacturer produces the popular Golf model?

11. What is the name of the luxury car division of Honda?

12. What does the acronym ABS stand for in regards to car safety?

13. Which car company produces the popular F-150 pickup truck?

14. What is the name of the all-electric car produced by Tesla?

15. What is the name of the British automaker that produces the MINI?

16. Which car company produces the popular Civic model?

17. What does the acronym RPM stand for in regards to a car's engine?

18. Which German automaker produces the popular 911 sports car?

19. What is the name of the all-wheel drive system used by Audi?

20. Which Japanese car manufacturer produces the popular Outlander model?

89. Holidays

1. What holiday is celebrated on December 25th?

2. What holiday is also known as All Hallows' Eve?

3. What holiday is celebrated on the fourth Thursday of November in the United States?

4. What holiday is celebrated on February 14th?

5. What holiday is celebrated on July 4th in the United States?

6. What holiday is celebrated on January 1st?

7. What holiday is celebrated on the second Monday of October in the United States?

8. What holiday is celebrated on November 2nd in Mexico?

9. What holiday is celebrated on the first Monday of September in the United States?

10. What holiday is celebrated on the third Monday of February in the United States?

11. What holiday is celebrated on April 1st?

12. What holiday is celebrated on the third Sunday of June in the United States?

13. What holiday is celebrated on the second Sunday of May in the United States?

14. What holiday is celebrated on December 31st?

15. What holiday is celebrated on the first Monday in May in the United States?

16. What holiday is celebrated on the third Thursday of November in the United States?

17. What holiday is celebrated on August 15th in some Christian countries?

18. What holiday is celebrated on the second Monday of October in Canada?

19. What holiday is celebrated on June 14th in the United States?

90. The Internet

1. What does the acronym HTTP stand for?

2. Who invented the World Wide Web?

3. What does the acronym HTML stand for?

4. What was the first popular web browser called?

5. What does the acronym SEO stand for?

6. What was the first video uploaded to YouTube?

7. What was the first ever email sent?

8. What is the most visited website in the world?
9. What does the acronym URL stand for?

10. What was the first social media platform launched?

11. What does the acronym ISP stand for?

12. What is the name of the first graphical web browser?

13. What does the acronym DNS stand for?

14. What is the most popular social media platform currently?

15. What is the name of the first website ever created?

16. What does the acronym VPN stand for?

17. What is the name of the first ever search engine?

18. What does the acronym IP stand for?

19. What is the name of the first ever e-commerce site?

20. What does the acronym CAPTCHA stand for?

91. Board Games

1. In which board game do players try to acquire property and charge rent to other players?

2. Which board game involves placing letter tiles on a board to create words?

3. In which game do players try to sink their opponent's ships by guessing their coordinates on a grid?

4. Which classic game involves capturing pieces on a checkered board and aiming to "checkmate" the opponent's king?

5. What board game is known for its colorful board and sliding tiles that can send players back to the start?

6. In which game do players use deductive reasoning to guess their opponent's hidden code?

7. What game involves moving pawns and other pieces around a board to reach the opposite end and "king" a piece?

8. Which game involves players drawing cards and trying to collect sets of four of the same kind?

9. What classic game is played with black and white stones on a grid, and aims to control more territory than the opponent?

10. Which game involves rolling dice and trying to reach the finish line with your pieces before your opponents?

11. What game involves building and strategically placing tiles to create a medieval landscape?

12. In which game do players take turns placing their colored pieces on a board, trying to surround and capture the opponent's pieces?

13. What game involves creating railway routes across North America to connect cities and earn points?

14. Which classic game involves moving pieces around a board and capturing the opponent's pieces by landing on them diagonally?

15. What game involves players taking turns rolling dice and moving their pieces around the board, trying to avoid traps and obstacles?

16. In which game do players use tiles to build and connect roads, cities, and farms in medieval Europe?

17. What game involves matching tiles with identical symbols to create a "hand" of four cards and score points?

18. Which game involves bluffing and trying to outwit your opponents by placing down tiles that may or may not match the current sequence?

19. In which game do players try to collect all the cards in the deck by asking their opponents for specific ranks?

20. What game involves drawing and guessing words with teammates to score points and advance on a board?

Answers

1. 1970s Movies Answers

1. Francis Ford Coppola.
2. Network.
3. Sylvester Stallone.
4. Alien.
5. The Way We Were.
6. Marlon Brando.
7. The Godfather Part II.
8. Wayne's World.
9. George Lucas.
10. The French Connection.
11. Saturday Night Fever.
12. Mark Hamill.
13. The French Connection.
14. Scarface.
15 Jaws.
16. Francis Ford Coppola.
17. Close Encounters of the Third Kind.
18. Taxi Driver.
19. Chinatown.
20. William Friedkin.

2. 1980s Movies Answers

1. DeLorean
2. Joshua
3. Harrison Ford

4. Claire Standish
5. Drew Barrymore
6. The Footloose
7. Inigo Montoya
8. Josh Baskin
9. Eddie Murphy
10. Maverick
11. Shermer High School
12. Bruce Willis
13. Ellen Ripley
14. Mr. Miyagi
15. Michael J. Fox
16. T-800
17. Mikey
18. Peter Weller
19. Falkor
20. Jean Marsh

3. 1990s Movies Answers

1. Kate Winslet
2. Lieutenant Dan Taylor.
3. Jodie Foster
4. Isla Nublar
5. Daniel Hillard/Mrs. Doubtfire
6. Vincent Vega
7. Leonardo DiCaprio
8. Mufasa
9. Neo
10. Tim Robbins
11. Captain Steven Hiller
12. Johnny Depp
13. Cher Horowitz
14. Kathy Bates
15. Lloyd Christmas
16. Elinor Dashwood
17. The T-1000
18. Anthony Hopkins
19. Casey Becker
20. Gary Trousdale and Kirk Wise

4. 2000s Movies Answers

1. "The Fellowship of the Ring"
2: North Shore High School
3. Johnny Depp
4. Ennis Del Mar
5. The Joker
6. Keanu Reeves
7. Juno MacGuff
8. Norman Osborn/Green Goblin
9. Michel Gondry
10. Ray Charles
11. Andy Serkis
12. Quidditch
13. Maggie Fitzgerald
14. Robert Langdon
15. Sacha Baron Cohen
16. Betty Elms/Diane Selwyn
17. Jason Bourne
18. Russell Crowe
19. The Parr family
20. Ridley Scott

5. 2010s Movies Answers

1. Stephen Hawking
2. Amy Poehler
3. Mia Dolan
4. Jesse Eisenberg
5. Jennifer Lawrence
6. Mark Watney
7. Jordan Peele
8. Christine "Lady Bird" McPherson
9. Wakanda
10. Robert Downey Jr.
11. Elsa
12. Daisy Ridley
13. Jordan Belfort
14. Amphibian Man

15. Joaquin Phoenix
16. Peter Parker/Spider-Man
17. Endurance
18. Alfonso Cuarón
19. W'Kabi
20. Sunnyside Daycare

6. 1980s TV Shows Answers

1. Colonel John "Hannibal" Smith
2. V.I.C.I. (Voice Input Child Identicant)
3. Advertising executive
4. Sam Malone
5. Thomas
6. Bayside High School
7. KITT (Knight Industries Two Thousand)
8. The Keaton family
9. Alex P. Keaton
10. Samantha Micelli
11. New York City High School for the Performing Arts
12. The Huxtable family
13. Tony Micelli
14. Rose Nylund
15. Steven Keaton
16. Arnold Jackson
17. David Addison Jr.
18. 21 Jump Street
19. Eastland School for Girls
20. Jesse Katsopolis.

7. 1990s TV Shows Answers

1. Central Perk
2. West Beverly Hills High School
3. Will Smith (the character's name was also Will Smith)
4. Mr. Belding
5. Twin Peaks, Washington
6. Rachel Green
7. Jerry Seinfeld (the character's name was also Jerry Seinfeld)
8. Buffy Summers

9. Fox Mulder
10. Dr. Frasier Crane
11. The Tanner family
12. Ally McBeal
13. Tim Taylor
14. Sabrina Spellman
15. Fran Fine
16. Carrie Bradshaw
17. John Adams High School
18. Dana Scully
19. Capeside, Massachusetts
20. Phoebe Buffay

8. 2000s TV Shows Answers

1. Bluth
2. Jon Hamm
3. Cheers
4. Lauren Graham
5. Dillon High School
6. Michael C. Hall
7. The Island
8. James Gandolfini
9. Central Perk
10. Sarah Jessica Parker
11. Harbor School
12. Steve Carell
13. Cage & Fish
14. Hugh Laurie
15. Fairview
16. Kiefer Sutherland
17. Seattle Grace Hospital
18. Bryan Cranston
19. Simpson
20. Tina Fey

9. Cartoon Characters Answers

1. Homer
2. Bugs Bunny.

3. The Joker.

4. Wile E. Coyote.

5. Nemo.

6. Timon.

7. Tom.

8. SpongeBob SquarePants.

9. Robin.

10. Tom.

10. 1990s Video Games Answers

1. Bowser.

2. Link.

3. Dr. Eggman (also known as Dr. Robotnik).

4. Doom.

5. Mario Kar

6. Earthbound (also known as Mother 2 in Japan).

7. Tetris.

8. Super Mario World 2: Yoshi's Island.

9. Street Fighter II.

10. Pokemon Red and Blue.

11. Crash Bandicoot.

12. Metal Gear Solid.

13. Tomb Raider.

14. Donkey Kong Country.

15. Final Fantasy VII.

16. Luigi's Mansion.

17. Sonic Adventure.

18. Space Quest VI: The Spinal Frontier.

19. Oddworld: Abe's Oddysee.

20. Legacy of Kain: Soul Reaver.

11. 2000s Video Games Answers

1. Half-Life 2.

2. Halo: Combat Evolved.

3. Chrono Trigger

4. Call of Duty: Black Ops.

5. Assassin's Creed.

6. Resident Evil 2.

7. Pokemon Diamond and Pearl.
8. God of War.
9. Fortnite.
10. Uncharted: Drake's Fortune.
11. Red Dead Redemption.
12. Super Mario Sunshine.
13. Tomb Raider: Legend.
14. Gears of War.
15. Ratchet & Clank.
16. Final Fantasy VII: Dirge of Cerberus.
17. Devil May Cry.
18. Gears of War 2.
19. Kingdom Hearts.
20. Assassin's Creed II.

12. Comic Book Characters Answers

1. Peter Parker
2. Bruce Wayne
3. Magneto
4. Krypton
5. Reverse-Flash
6. Doctor Doom
7. Pepper Potts
8. Venom
9. Alan Moore
10. Hal Jordan
11. The Joker
12. Thor
13. Professor Xavier
14. Mary Jane Watson
15. Steve Rogers
16. Wilson Fisk (Kingpin)
17. Klyntar
18. Shredder
19. Daredevil
20. Thanos.

13. Comic Book Superheroes And Their Abilities Answers

2. The Declaration of Independence.

3. George Washington.

4. The Battle of Saratoga.

5. General Charles Cornwallis.

6. Thomas Paine.

7. The Treaty of Paris.

8. The Culper Spy Ring.

9. Hessians.

10. John Paul Jones.

17. French and Indian War Answers

1. 1754.

2. General Edward Braddock.

3. Competition between France and Great Britain for land in North America.

4. Fort Duquesne.

5. Fort Necessity.

6. Pontiac.

7. Treaty of Paris.

8. Quebec.

9. William Pitt.

10. Battle of the Monongahela.

11. Marquis de Montcalm.

12. Iroquois.

13. James Abercrombie.

14. John Forbes.

15. George Washington.

16. John Bradstreet.

17. Louis-Joseph de Montcalm.

18. Fort Carillon (later renamed Fort Ticonderoga).

19. James Wolfe.

20. The Ohio River.

18. The Civil War Answers

1. 1861.

2. Jefferson Davis.

3. Abraham Lincoln.

4. Robert E. Lee.

5. George McClellan.

6. The First Battle of Bull Run.

7. The Gettysburg Address.

8. The Battle of Antietam.

9. The CSS Hunley.

10. William Tecumseh Sherman.

11. Andersonville.

12. Robert E. Lee.

13. Ulysses S. Grant.

14. William Tecumseh Sherman.

15. Robert E. Lee.

16. Clara Barton.

17. Abraham Lincoln.

18. Stand Watie.

19. The CSS Virginia

20. Douglas MacArthur

19. World War 1 Answers

1. 1914.

2. The Triple Alliance.

3. The Triple Entente.

4. The Schlieffen Plan.

5. The Lusitania.

6. The Treaty of Versailles.

7. Gavrilo Princip.

8. The Second Battle of Ypres.

9. The Spring Offensive.

10. The First Battle of the Marne.

11. John J. Pershing.

12. Manfred von Richthofen, also known as the "Red Baron."

13. Florence Nightingale.

14. The Treaty of Brest-Litovsk.

15. The Battle of the Somme.

16. The SMS Derfflinger.

17. The Battle of Belleau Wood.

18. "In Flanders Fields."

19. Grigori Rasputin.

20. The Treaty of Saint-Germain-en-Laye.

20. World War 2 answers

1. 1939.
2. Adolf Hitler.
3. Appeasement.
4. The Molotov-Ribbentrop Pact.
5. The Battle of Stalingrad.
6. The Battle of Midway.
7. The Enigma machine.
8. The Yalta Conference.
9. Auschwitz.
10. D-Day.
11. The Battle of Kursk.
12. The Manhattan Project.
13. Raising the Flag on Iwo Jima.
14. The Luftwaffe.
15. The Battle of Berlin.
16. The Treaty of San Francisco.
17. Winston Churchill.
18. Emperor Hirohito.
19. The Battle of Iwo Jima.
20. The Potsdam Conference.

21. The Vietnam War Answers

1. 1955.
2. The Viet Cong.
3. The Gulf of Tonkin Resolution.
4. Operation Rolling Thunder.
5. Ho Chi Minh.
6. Daniel Ellsberg.
7. The My Lai Massacre.
8. Agent Orange.
9. The Battle of Khe Sanh.
10. General William Westmoreland.
11. John Ripley.
12. John McCain.
13. Michael Herr.
14. Desmond Doss.
15. Harry Kinnard.
16. The Battle of Ia Drang.

17. Ngo Dinh Diem.
18. Captain Willard.
19. Bruce Crandall.
20. The Paris Peace Accords.

22. US Presidents And The Time They Served Answers

1. 1789-1797
2. 1797-1801
3. 1801-1809
4. 1809-1817
5. 1817-1825
6. 1825-1829
7. 1829-1837
8. 1837-1841
9. 1841
10. 1841-1845
11. 1845-1849
12. 1849-1850
13. 1850-1853
14. 1853-1857
15. 1857-1861
16. 1861-1865
17. 1865-1869
18. 1869-1877
19. 1877-1881
20. 1881 Note: James A. Garfield only served from March 4, 1881 until his death on September 19, 1881,.
21. 1913-1921
22. 1921-1923
23. 1923-1929
24. 1929-1933
24. 1945-1953
26. 1953-1961
27. 1961-1963
28. 1963-1969
29. 1969-1974
30. 1974-1977

23. Famous Artists And Their Work Answers

1. Leonardo da Vinci
2. Michelangelo
3. Vincent van Gogh
4. Pablo Picasso
5. Rembrandt
6. Johannes Vermeer
7. Claude Monet
8. Salvador Dali
9. Edvard Munch
10. Auguste Rodin
11. Wassily Kandinsky
12. Georgia O'Keeffe
13. Henri Matisse
14. Sandro Botticelli
15. Jackson Pollock
16. Paul Cézanne
17. Gustav Klimt
18. Edward Hopper
19. Marc Chagall
20. Frida Kahlo

24. Famous Songs And Their Creators Answers

1. Freddie Mercury
2. Jimmy Page and Robert Plant
3. Bob Dylan
4. Kurt Cobain, Krist Novoselic, and Dave Grohl
5. Paul McCartney
6. Jimi Hendrix
7. John Lennon
8. Axl Rose, Slash, Izzy Stradlin, Duff McKagan, and Steven Adler
9. Michael Jackson
10. Dolly Parton
11. Don Henley, Glenn Frey, and Don Felder
12. Rod Temperton
13. Paul Simon
14. James Horner and Will Jennings
15. Pål Waaktaar-Savoy, Morten Harket, and Magne Furuholmen
16. Mick Jagger and Keith Richards

17. Leonard Cohen
18. Paul McCartney
19. Queen and David Bowie

25. Famous Poems And Their Authors Answers

1. T.S. Eliot
2. Allen Ginsberg
3. John Keats
4. Dylan Thomas
5. Robert Frost
6. Edgar Allan Poe
7. Edgar Allan Poe
8. William Blake
9. John Keats
10. William Shakespeare
11. Rudyard Kipling
12. Alfred, Lord Tennyson
13. Percy Bysshe Shelley
14. Andrew Marvell
15. Wilfred Owen
16. Lewis Carroll
17. T.S. Eliot
18. William Carlos Williams
19. Robert Frost
20. William Shakespeare

26. Inventors And What They Invented Answers

1. Thomas Edison
2. Alexander Graham Bell
3. Nikola Tesla
4. Eli Whitney
5. Louis Pasteur
6. Benjamin Franklin
7. Johannes Gutenberg
8. Guglielmo Marconi
9. Orville and Wilbur Wright
10. Samuel Morse
11. James Watt

12. Charles Babbage
13. Karl Benz
14. John Logie Baird
15. Tim Berners-Lee
16. Steve Jobs
17. Jonas Salk
18. Grace Hopper
19. Louis Braille
20. Stephanie Kwolek

27. Famous Books And Their Authors Answers

1. Harper Lee
2. George Orwell
3. Jane Austen
4. J.D. Salinger
5. F. Scott Fitzgerald
6. J.R.R. Tolkien
7. C.S. Lewis
8. Mark Twain
9. Lewis Carroll
10. Aldous Huxley
11. Mary Shelley
12. Oscar Wilde
13. Herman Melville
14. Nathaniel Hawthorne
15. John Steinbeck
16. Gabriel García Márquez
17. Alice Walker
18. Charles Dickens
19. Mark Twain
20. Leo Tolstoy
21. Ernest Hemingway
22. Emily Bronte
23. J.R.R. Tolkien
24. Charlotte Bronte
25. Jane Austen
26. S.E. Hinton
27. Ernest Hemingway
28. Frances Hodgson Burnett

29. Anne Frank
30. William Faulkner

28. Famous Movies And Their Directors Answers

1. Francis Ford Coppola
2. Quentin Tarantino
3. James Cameron
4. Steven Spielberg
5. Frank Darabont
6. Jonathan Demme
7. George Lucas
8. Victor Fleming
9. Peter Jackson
10. Martin Scorsese
11. The Wachowski Brothers
12. Steven Spielberg
13. Michael Curtiz
14. William Friedkin
15. Victor Fleming
16. Alfred Hitchcock
17. Steven Spielberg
18. Stanley Kubrick
19. Ridley Scott
20. Stanley Kubrick

29. Famous People Answers

1. George Washington.
2. Albert Einstein.
3. Queen Victoria.
4. J.K. Rowling.
5. Martin Luther King Jr.
6. Leonardo da Vinci.
7. Abraham Lincoln.
8. Napoleon Bonaparte.
9. Thomas Edison.
10. Wolfgang Amadeus Mozart.

30. Famous Quotes And The People Who Said Them Answers

1. Steve Jobs
2. Robert Frost
3. Martin Luther King Jr.
4. Albert Einstein
5. Nelson Mandela
6. Mahatma Gandhi
7. Socrates
8. Thomas Edison
9. Franklin D. Roosevelt
10. Walt Disney
11. Eleanor Roosevelt
12. Confucius
13. Wayne Gretzky
14. Nelson Mandela
15. Socrates
16. Henry Ford
17. Charles R. Swindoll
18. Albert Einstein
19. Peter Drucker
20. Winston Churchill

31. Julius Caesar Answers

1. 44 BC.
2. Rome
3. Gaius Julius Caesar.
4. He was a consul.
5. Mark Antony and Lepidus.
6. The Battle of Pharsalus.
7. The Rubicon River.
8. Brutus and Cassius.
9. Cleopatra.
10. Julius Caesar himself.
11. Octavian, later known as Augustus.
12. William Shakespeare.
13. Dictator for Life.
14. Cornelia and Calpurnia.
15. The Feast of Anna Perenna.
16. Suetonius.

17. Marcus Junius Brutus.
18. Incitatus.
19. The Gallic Wars.
20. Pompey.

32. William Shakespeare Answers

1. Romeo and Juliet.
2. Stratford-upon-Avon.
3. Hamlet.
4. The Merchant of Venice.
5. The Tempest.
6. Macbeth.
7. Romeo and Juliet.
8. Hamlet.
9. Othello.
10. A Midsummer Night's Dream.
11. As You Like It.
12. As You Like It.
13. The Taming of the Shrew.
14. Othello.
15. The Tempest.
16. Twelfth Night.
17. The Merchant of Venice.
18. A Midsummer Night's Dream.
19. Antony and Cleopatra.
20. Henry IV, Part 1 and Henry IV, Part 2.

33. Napoleon Bonaparte Answers

1. 1769
2. Ajaccio, Corsica
3. Napoléon Bonaparte
4. 5 feet 6.5 inches (1.69 meters)
5. Joséphine de Beauharnais
6. 1804
7. The Battle of Waterloo
8. The Duke of Wellington
9. The island of Elba
10. Marie Louise of Austria

11. Tesla was a strong advocate for renewable energy sources, particularly hydropower and solar energy.
12. Tesla died of heart failure in New York City in 1943.
13. The Tesla Roadster is an all-electric sports car developed by Tesla Motors, named in honor of Nikola Tesla.
14. The Tesla Science Center at Wardenclyffe was a project to restore and preserve Tesla's Wardenclyffe Tower as a museum and center for scientific research and education.
15. The War of Currents was a historical event in which Thomas Edison and George Westinghouse battled over the future of the electrical system, with Tesla's alternating current eventually winning out.
16. Tesla disagreed with Einstein's theory of relativity, arguing that it was incomplete and inaccurate.
17. Tesla's most significant contribution to the field of electrical engineering was the development of the alternating current (AC) electrical system.
18. The Tesla unit is a measurement of magnetic flux density, named in honor of Nikola Tesla.
19. The Tesla Award is a prestigious engineering award given by the Institute of Electrical and Electronics Engineers (IEEE) for significant contributions to the field of electrical engineering.
20. Tesla believed that wireless transmission of power was possible, and conducted extensive research into the subject. However, his ideas were never fully realized during his lifetime.

37. Ruth Bader Ginsburg Answers

1. Joan Ruth Bader
2. 1933
3. New York
4. 1993
5. President Bill Clinton
6. Judge on the U.S. Court of Appeals for the District of Columbia Circuit
7. The Notorious RBG
8. Women's rights and gender equality
9. Reed v. Reed, which challenged the constitutionality of a law that gave preference to men over women in estate matters
10. She voted in favor of the majority decision, which legalized abortion nationwide
11. 2015 case Obergefell v. Hodges, which legalized same-sex marriage nationwide
12. Pancreatic cancer
13. Harvard Law School
14. Cornell University
15. The Presidential Medal of Freedom
16. She was opposed to the death penalty and believed it violated the Eighth Amendment's prohibition of cruel and unusual punishment.

17. The Fourteenth Amendment, which guarantees equal protection under the law
18. "My Own Words," a collection of her writings and speeches
19. Hebrew
20. 2020

38. Queen Elizabeth I Answers

1. King Henry VIII
2. The Virgin Queen
3. Queen Mary I
4. The Spanish Armada
5. James Hamilton
6. Anne Boleyn
7. Mary, Queen of Scots
8. Will Sommers
9. William Shakespeare
10. William Cecil
11. The Northern Rebellion
12. Robert Devereux, 2nd Earl of Essex
13. Sir Francis Drake
14. Sir Francis Drake
15. Robert Dudley, Earl of Leicester
16. King James I (James VI of Scotland)
17. Robert Devereux, 2nd Earl of Essex
18. Mary, Queen of Scots
19. The Act of Supremacy
20. Catherine of Aragon

39. Cleopatra Answers

1. Cleopatra was of Greek-Macedonian ancestry.
2. Cleopatra's parents were Ptolemy XII Auletes and possibly Cleopatra V Tryphaena.
3. Cleopatra was the last
4. Cleopatra's most famous lovers were Julius Caesar and Mark Antony.
5. Cleopatra's first language was Greek.
6. Cleopatra's famous barge was called the Antonia.
7. Cleopatra had four children, three with Mark Antony and one with Julius Caesar.
8. Cleopatra's personal physician was named Olympos.
9. Cleopatra died by suicide, most likely by poisoning herself with a toxic snake.

10. The location of Cleopatra's tomb is unknown, although it is believed to be in or near Alexandria.

11. The book is titled "Cleopatra: A Life."

12. The movie is simply titled "Cleopatra."

13. Ptolemy XIII was Cleopatra's younger brother and husband, as it was common for members of the Ptolemaic dynasty to marry siblings to maintain power.

14. Cleopatra's loyal servant and handmaiden was named Charmian.

15. Cleopatra fought alongside Mark Antony in the Battle of Actium, which they lost to Octavian (later known as Caesar Augustus).

16. Cleopatra famously wore a boat-shaped headdress adorned with pearls and other precious stones.

17. The Roman general who defeated Cleopatra and Mark Antony was Caesar Augustus.

18. Cleopatra gained control of Egypt by aligning herself with Julius Caesar, who helped her defeat her brother in a civil war.

19. Cleopatra was 18 years old when she became ruler of Egypt.

20. Cleopatra's full name was Cleopatra VII Philopator.

40. Genghis Khan Answers

1. Temujin
2. 1206
3. Borte
4. Urgench
5. Jin Dynasty
6. Chagatai
7. Nasir al-Din al-Tusi
8. Karakorum
9. Two
10. Jalal ad-Din
11. Wanyan Yongji
12. Bukhara
13. Subutai
14. Ogodei Khan
15. The Art of War by Sun Tzu
16. Liu Ting
17. Sultanate of Rum
18. The Mongol Imperial Guard
19. Kiev
20. Subutai

41. Che Guevara Answers

1. Ernesto "Che" Guevara de la Serna
2. Argentina
3. Fidel Castro
4. Cuba
5. Minister of Industry
6. Bolivia
7. He was captured and executed by the Bolivian army in 1967.
8. The Motorcycle Diaries
9. Havana, Cuba
10. Guerrillero Heroico
11. "Until victory, always"
12. Cuba
13. Che Guevara: A Revolutionary Life
14. The Problems of the War and Peace in Our Time
15. Versos Sencillos by José Martí
16. The 26th of July Movement
17. 1968
18. La Higuera
19. Steven Soderbergh
20. Simón Bolívar

42. Confucius Answers

1. Confucius was a Chinese philosopher, politician, and teacher who lived from 551-479 BCE.
2. Confucius' real name was Kong Qiu.
3. The philosophy of Confucius is called Confucianism.
4. Confucius' most famous book is called "The Analects."
5. The central idea of Confucianism is the importance of moral values and ethics.
6. The five key relationships in Confucianism are between ruler and subject, father and son, elder and younger brother, husband and wife, and friend and friend.
7. Education was highly valued in Confucianism, and it was seen as a means of improving oneself and society as a whole.
8. Confucianism believed in the importance of good government and politics, and emphasized the role of virtuous leaders.
9. Confucianism generally placed women in subordinate roles to men, but also emphasized the importance of filial piety and respect for one's parents.
10. Confucius lived most of his life in the state of Lu, in what is now eastern China.

11. "Junzi" is a term in Confucianism that refers to a person who is noble, upright, and morally superior.
12. The Confucian ideal of the "gentleman" was a person who was well-educated, cultured, and morally upright.
13. Confucianism generally discouraged war and violence, and emphasized the importance of peace and harmony.
14. Ritual was seen as a means of promoting social harmony and reinforcing moral values in Confucianism.
15. Confucianism did not emphasize religious belief as much as moral values and ethics.
16. Confucianism placed a great deal of importance on the family, and emphasized the role of filial piety and respect for one's parents.
17. Confucianism emphasized the importance of social harmony and mutual respect, regardless of social class.
18. Confucianism placed a great deal of value on knowledge and education, and emphasized the importance of learning throughout one's life.
19. Confucianism valued the arts as a means of promoting moral values and cultivating one's character.
20. Confucianism has had a lasting impact on Chinese society, influencing everything from politics to education to family life. It remains an important cultural

43. Winston Churchill Answers

1. Winston Leonard Spencer-Churchill.
2. First Lord of the Admiralty.
3. World War II.
4. Oxfordshire, England.
5. "We shall fight on the beaches, we shall fight on the landing grounds, we shall fight in the fields and in the streets, we shall fight in the hills; we shall never surrender."
6. 1953.
7. Conservative Party.
8. Franklin D. Roosevelt.
9. The "Iron Curtain."
10. Two.
11. Whiskey.
12. Chancellor of the Exchequer.
13. Writing.
14. "Special Relationship."
15. The Churchill family.
16. Clementine Churchill.
17. The Second Boer War.

18. Depression.
19. 50.
20. The index and middle fingers.

44. Alexander The Great Answers

1. 356 BC.
2. Philip II.
3. 20 years old.
4. Bucephalus.
5. Aristotle.
6. Darius III.
7. Alexandria.
8. 323 BC.
9. The exact cause is unknown, but it is believed that he died of either malaria or alcohol poisoning.
10. "King of Kings."
11. Hephaestion.
12. Bucephala.
13. Porus.
14. The Battle of the Hydaspes.
15. The Speech of Alexander the Great at Opis.
16. Arrian.
17. The Siege of Tyre.
18. The Indus River.
19. Roxana.
20. Ptolemy I Soter.

45. Joan Of Arc Answers

1. 1412.
2. The Maid of Orleans.
3. The Hundred Years' War.
4. Saints and angels
5. 17.
6. Charles VII.
7. The Trial of Condemnation.
8. Rouen.
9. Pope Callixtus III.
10. Joan of Arc.

11. Saint Joan.

12. She was burned at the stake.

13. Gilles de Rais.

14. The Sword of Saint Catherine.

15. To drive the English out of France and help crown Charles VII as king.

16. A white dove holding a sword.

17. About a year.

18. Pierre Cauchon.

19. Henry VI.

20. It was a turning point in the Hundred Years' War and paved the way for French victories over the English.

46. Animals Answers

1. The bumblebee bat (also known as Kitti's hog-nosed bat)

2. The giraffe

3. The hummingbird

4. The blue whale

5. The ostrich

6. The cheetah

7. The sloth

8. The chameleon

9. The saltwater crocodile

10. The bee hummingbird

11. The ocean quahog (a type of clam)

12. The bat

13. The African elephant

14. The whale shark

15. The opossum

16. The sailfish

17. The sloth

18. The capybara

19. The zebra

20. The spectacled bear.

47. Insects Answers

1. Firefly

2. Fairyfly

3. Pillbug (also known as roly-poly)

4. Bees

5. Mantodea

6. Ants

7. Monarch butterfly

8. 6-8 weeks

9. Spittlebug

10. Bedbug

11. Chameleon

12. Bumblebee

13. Click beetle

14. Blattodea

15. Flea

16. Spider

17. Atlas moth

18. Dragonfly

19. Assassin bug

20. Cicada

48. Dogs Answers

1. Labrador Retriever.

2. Chihuahua.

3. Great Dane.

4. Golden Retriever.

5. Bulldog.

6. Chow Chow.

7. Greyhound.

8. Bella.

9. Scottish Terrier

10. Dachshund.

11. Poodle.

12. German Shepherd.

13. Havanese.

14. Akita.

15. Dalmatian.

16. Pug.

17. The Chihuahua.

18. Belgian Malinois.

19. Laika, a mixed breed stray dog.

20. The Tibetan Mastiff.

49. Cats Answers

1. Felis catus
2. Five
3. Manx
4. A clowder or a glaring
5. Smell
6. About 9 weeks
7. Puss
8. Cheshire Cat
9. Garfield
10. Persian
11. Cats
12. The Cat in the Hat
13. Duchess
14. Erwin Schrödinger
15. Jiji
16. Mr. Mistoffelees
17. Siamese
18. Firestar
19. Tom
20. Garfield

50. Elephants Answers

1. Elephant
2. 11,000 lbs (5,000 kg)
3. 6,000 lbs (2,700 kg)
4. 26
5. 60-70 years
6. 22 months
7. A herd
8. Bull
9. Cow
10. Calf
11. Loxodonta africana or Elephas maximus depending on the species
12. 2 - African and Asian
13. African elephants are larger with bigger ears and tusks that both male and female elephants have. Asian elephants are smaller with smaller ears and only male elephants have tusks.

14. Up to 300 pounds (136 kg) of food per day

15. Leaves, bark, fruits, and vegetables.

16. Over 40,000

17. Up to 25 mph (40 km/h)

18. Yes, they are excellent swimmers and can swim long distances.

19. Through a variety of vocalizations, body language, and even infrasonic sounds that are too low for humans to hear.

20. Yes, both African and Asian elephants are listed as vulnerable or endangered due to habitat loss, poaching, and other threats.

51. Turtles Answers

1. Testudines

2. About 300 species

3. The leatherback sea turtle

4. The speckled padloper tortoise

5. No, they have a beak instead

6. Some species of turtles can hold their breath for several hours

7. They retreat into their shells

8. 188 years

9. Tortoises are land-dwelling while turtles are aquatic

10. Leonardo

11. The giraffe-necked turtle

12. The alligator snapping turtle

13. Female turtles dig a hole in the ground with their hind legs and lay their eggs

14. Depending on the species, turtles can be herbivores, carnivores, or omnivores

15. "The Tale of Peter Rabbit" by Beatrix Potter

16. Yes, they can

17. Franklin the Turtle

18. Kemp's ridley sea turtle

19. Yes, they have internal ears

20. Depending on the species, turtles can run up to 10 miles per hour

52. Fish Answers

1. Cod

2. The Atlantic Herring

3. Tuna or Salmon

4. Nemo (from Finding Nemo)

5. Pike

6. Tuna

7. Coho salmon

8. Pufferfish (also known as Fugu)

9. Lungfish

10. Smoked haddock

11. Salmon roe (Ikura)

12. Flatfish (such as flounder or sole)

13. Catfish

14. Haddock

15. Sea bass

16. Salmon

17. Turbot

18. Skate

19. Sockeye salmon

20. Rainbowfish

53. Sharks Answers

1. There are over 500 species of sharks.
2. The whale shark is the largest species of shark, growing up to 40 feet in length.
3. The shortfin mako shark can swim up to 60 miles per hour, making it the fastest species of shark.
4. The dwarf lanternshark is the smallest species of shark, growing to only 8 inches in length.
5. The hammerhead shark is known for its distinctive head shape.
6. The great white shark is the largest predatory fish in the ocean.
7. The great white shark is sometimes referred to as the "sea tiger."
dinosaurs
8. The tiger shark is known for its long, pointed snout and serrated teeth.
9. The great white shark is considered the most dangerous species of shark to humans.
10. The mako shark is known for jumping out of the water.
11. The largest shark ever recorded was a female whale shark that measured 41.5 feet in length.
12. The leopard shark is known for its unique pattern of spots.
13. The bull shark is known for its ability to live in both saltwater and freshwater.
14. The blacktip shark is known for its distinctive black tip on its fins.
16. The blue shark is known for its long, narrow body and ability to swim at high speeds.
17. The lantern shark is known for its ability to produce a glowing blue-green light.
18. The frilled shark is known for its prehistoric appearance.
19. The sawfish is known for its saw-like snout and ability to sense electrical fields.
20. The thresher shark is known for its long, slender body and ability to swim great distances.

54. Dinosaurs Answers

1. Argentinosaurus
2. Microraptor
3. Suchomimus
4. Triceratops
5. Diplodocus
6. Velociraptor
7. Pterodactyl
8. Ankylosaurus
9. Cryolophosaurus
10. Stegosaurus
11. Styracosaurus
12. Spinosaurus
13. Dimetrodon
14. Deinocheirus
15. Einiosaurus
16. Tyrannosaurus Rex
17. Coelophysis
18. Hadrosaurus
19. Sauroposeidon

55. Phobias Answers

1. Arachnophobia
2. Acrophobia
3. Agoraphobia
4. Claustrophobia
5. Ophidiophobia
6. Coulrophobia
7. Astraphobia
8. Trypophobia
9. Hydrophobia
10. Hemophobia
11. Nyctophobia
12. Pteromerhanophobia
13. Thanatophobia.
14. Xenophobia
15. Glossophobia
16. Mysophobia

17. Athazagoraphobia
18. Ablutophobia
19. Triskaidekaphobia
20. Cynophobia

56. Saturn Answers

1. It is the sixth planet from the Sun.
2. Titan.
3. Its magnificent ring system.
4. It has 82 confirmed moons.
5. Cassini.
6. It takes about 10.7 Earth hours to complete one rotation on its axis.
7. It takes about 29.5 Earth years to orbit the Sun.
8. It is about 886 million miles (1.4 billion kilometers).
9. The surface temperature of Saturn is about -288 degrees Fahrenheit (-178 degrees Celsius).
10. Saturn is about nine times larger than Earth.
11. Hydrogen and helium.
12. The Cassini Division.
13. The Saturn Hexagon.
14. The Great White Spot.
15. Rhea.
16. Aegaeon.
17. Enceladus.
18. Hyperion.
19. Phoebe.
20. Dragonfly.

57. Jupiter Answers

1. It is the fifth planet from the Sun.
2. Ganyme
3. The Great Red Spot, a giant storm that has been raging for at least 350 years.
4. It has 79 confirmed moons.
5. Juno.
6. It takes about 9.9 Earth hours to complete one rotation on its axis.
7. It takes about 11.9 Earth years to orbit the Sun.
8. It is about 484 million miles (778 million kilometers).
9. The surface temperature of Jupiter is about -234 degrees Fahrenheit (-145 degrees Celsius).
10. Jupiter is about 11 times larger than Earth.

11. Hydrogen and helium.
12. Ganymede.
13. Callisto.
14. Io.
15. Europa.
16. Galileo.
17. Galileo.
18. Hubble Space Telescope
19. Europa Clipper.
20. 4 Vesta.

58. Space Answers

1. The Milky Way.
2. 93 million miles (149.6 million kilometers).
3. Jupiter.
4. Neil Armstrong.
5. Sputnik 1.
6. Kathryn D. Sullivan.
7. Explorer 6.
8. Hubble Space Telescope.
9. Voyager 1.
10. Cassini-Huygens.
11. Mars Perseverance.
12. Aurora Borealis.
13. Aurora Australis.
14. SpaceX Dragon.
15. Beresheet.
16. Ceres.
17. Sirius.
18. Ursa Minor.
19. New Horizons.
20. Artemis

59. The Universe Answers

1. 13.8 billion years.
2. The Big Bang theory.
3. Dark energy.
4. The Hercules-Corona Borealis Great Wall.

5. Sagittarius A*.
6. UY Scuti.
7. 51 Pegasi b.
8. The multiverse theory.
9. Nuclear fusion.
10. The Canis Major Dwarf Galaxy.
11. Voyager 1.
12. Supernova.
13. Gravity.
14. The Andromeda Galaxy.
15. The Hubble Space Telescope.
16. Black hole.
17. Kepler.
18. Ursa Major.
19. NGC 1277.
20. Euclid.

60. Famous Athletes Answers

1. Usain Bolt.
2. Michael Jordan.
3. Kareem Abdul-Jabbar.
4. Jack Nicklaus.
5. Michael Phelps.
6. Rod Laver.
7. Simone Biles.
8. Lionel Messi.
9. Tom Brady.
10. Dominique Dawes.
11. Hakeem Olajuwon.
12. Steffi Graf.
13. Manny Pacquiao.
14. Pelé.
15. Althea Gibson.
16. Michael Owen.
17. Bill Russell.
18. Tonya Harding.
19. Abby Wambach.
20. LeBron James.

61. Soccer/Football Answers

1. France
2. Alan Shearer
3. The Pittsburgh Steelers and the New England Patriots (6)
4. Uruguay
5. Robert Lewandowski
6. Alan Shearer (with 34 goals)
7. Chelsea
8. George Weah
9. Pelé
10. Soviet Union
11. Real Madrid (13)
12. Lionel Messi
13. Uruguay
14. Lionel Messi
15. Manchester City
16. United States
17. Lionel Messi (with 7)
18. Portugal
19. Silvio Piola
20. Brazil (5)

62. NFL Answers

1. Arizona Cardinals (founded in 1898 as the Morgan Athletic Club)
2. New England Patriots (6)
3. Tom Brady
4. New England Patriots (21 consecutive wins, spanning the 2003-2004 seasons)
5. Emmitt Smith
6. Chicago Bears (34 players)
7. Tom Brady
8. Green Bay Packers
9. Pittsburgh Steelers
10. Peyton Manning
11. Tampa Bay Buccaneers
12. Jerry Rice
13. Green Bay Packers (13)
14. O.J. Simpson
15. Miami Dolphins (1972)

16. Marcus Allen
17. Dallas Cowboys (8)
18. Paul Krause
19. Oakland Raiders (Super Bowl XV)
20. Bruce Smith

63. Basketball Answers

1. The 1971-72 Los Angeles Lakers
2. Kareem Abdul-Jabbar
3. Milwaukee Bucks
4. Stephen Curry
5. Wilt Chamberlain (100 points)
6. The 1995-96 Chicago Bulls
7. Bill Russell
8. Wilt Chamberlain
9. Bill Russell (11 championships)
10. LeBron James
11. Boston Celtics (17)
12. John Stockton
13. Kareem Abdul-Jabbar
14. Michael Jordan
15. Boston Celtics (8 championships, from 1959 to 1966)
16. Wilt Chamberlain
17. John Stockton
18. The 1971-72 Los Angeles Lakers (33 consecutive wins)
19. Magic Johnson
20. Michael Jordan (6)

64. Baseball Answers

1. Pete Rose (4,256 hits)
2. Alex Rodriguez
3. Tom Cheney (21 strikeouts)
4. The 1906 Chicago White Sox
5. Frank Robinson
6. Nolan Ryan (5,714 strikeouts)
7. Catcher
8. Barry Bonds (73 home runs in 2001)
9. Cy Young (511 wins)

10. Jackie Robinson
11. Stan Musial (3,630 hits with the St. Louis Cardinals)
12. The Oakland Athletics (Philadelphia, Kansas City, Oakland, and Los Angeles)
13. Greg Maddux
14. Sammy Sosa (20 home runs in June 1998)
15. Bobby Richardson
16. Nolan Ryan (7 no-hitters)
17. New York Yankees (27 championships)
18. Carlton Fisk
19. Rickey Henderson (130 stolen bases in 1982)
20. Ed Walsh (1.82 ERA)

65. NFL Teams And The Cities and States They Are From Answers

1. Glendale, Arizona
2. Atlanta, Georgia
3. Baltimore, Maryland
4. Orchard Park, New York
5. Charlotte, North Carolina
6. Chicago, Illinois
7. Cincinnati, Ohio
8. Cleveland, Ohio
9. Arlington, Texas
10. Denver, Colorado
11. Detroit, Michigan
12. Green Bay, Wisconsin
13. Houston, Texas
14. Indianapolis, Indiana
15. Jacksonville, Florida
16. Kansas City, Missouri
17. Las Vegas, Nevada
18. Inglewood, California
19. Inglewood, California
20. Miami Gardens, Florida
21. Minneapolis, Minnesota
22. Foxborough, Massachusetts
23. New Orleans, Louisiana
24. East Rutherford, New Jersey
25. East Rutherford, New Jersey
26. Philadelphia, Pennsylvania

27. Pittsburgh, Pennsylvania
28. Santa Clara, California
29. Seattle, Washington
30. Tampa, Florida
31. Nashville, Tennessee
32. Landover, Maryland

66. Geography Answers

1. The Eiffel Tower
2. The Great Pyramid of Giza
3. The Taj Mahal
4. Stonehenge
5. Times Square
6. Disneyland
7. The Golden Gate Bridge
8. Niagara Falls
9. St. Peter's Basilica
10. The Kremlin
11. Walt Disney World
12. The Grand Canyon
13. The Sydney Opera House
14. The Tower of London
15. The Trevi Fountain
16. The Louvre
17. The Palace of Versailles
18. The Washington Monument
19. The Burj Al Arab
20. Maracanã Stadium

67. National Parks In The United States With Their Respective States Answers

1. Maine
2. Utah
3. South Dakota
4. Texas
5. Utah
6. Utah
7. Utah
8. California

9. Oregon
10. California and Nevada
11. Alaska
12. Florida
13. Alaska
14. Montana
15. Arizona
16. Wyoming
17. Tennessee and North Carolina
18. California
19. Alaska
20. California
21. California
22. Washington
23. Arizona
24. California
25. Colorado
26. California
27. Wyoming, Montana, and Idaho
28. California
29. Utah
30. Minnesota

68. Countries And Their Leaders Answers

1. United States
2. United Kingdom
3. France
4. Germany
5. Russia
6. China
7. Japan
8. South Korea
9. Brazil
10. Mexico
11. Canada
12. India
13. Pakistan
14. Australia
15. New Zealand

16. South Africa
17. Nigeria
18. Saudi Arabia
19. Iran
20. Israel

69. U.S. States And Their Capitals Answers

1. Montgomery
2. Juneau
3. Phoenix
4. Little Rock
5. Sacramento
6. Denver
7. Hartford
8. Dover
9. Tallahassee
10. Atlanta
11. Honolulu
12. Boise
13. Springfield
14. Indianapolis
15. Des Moines
16. Topeka
17. Frankfort
18. Baton Rouge
19. Augusta
20. Annapolis
21 Boston
22. Lansing
23. St. Paul
24. Jackson
25. Jefferson City
26. Helena
27. Lincoln
28. Carson City
29. Concord
30. Trenton
31. Santa Fe
32. Albany

33. Raleigh
34. Bismarck
35. Columbus
36. Oklahoma City
37. Salem
38. Harrisburg
39. Providence
a 40. Columbia
41. Pierre
42 Nashville
43. Austin
44. Salt Lake City
45. Montpelier
46. Richmond
47. Olympia
48. Charleston
49. Madison
50. Cheyenne

70. Countries With Their Capitals Answers

1. Kabul
2. Buenos Aires
3. Canberra
4. Brasilia
5. Ottawa
6. Beijing
7. Copenhagen
8. Cairo
9. Paris
10. Berlin
11. Athens
12. New Delhi
13. Tehran
14. Baghdad
15. Dublin
16. Jerusalem
7. Rome
18. Tokyo
19. Nairobi

20. Mexico City
21. Amsterdam
22. Abuja
23. Oslo
24. Islamabad
25. Lima
26. Manila
27. Warsaw
28, Moscow
29. Riyadh
30. Pretoria (administrative); Cape Town (legislative); Bloemfontein (judiciary)
31. Seoul
32. Madrid
33. Stockholm
34. Bern
35. Bangkok
36. Ankara
37. London
38. Washington D.C.
39. Caracas
40. Hanoi

71. Countries In Asia Answers

1. Afghanistan
2. Armenia
3. Azerbaijan
4. Bahrain
5. Bangladesh
6. Bhutan
7. Brunei
8. Cambodia
9. China
10. Cyprus
11. Georgia
12. India
13. Indonesia
14. Iran
15. Iraq
16. Israel

17. Japan

18. Jordan

19. Kazakhstan

20. Kuwait

21. Kyrgyzstan

22. Laos

23. Lebanon

24. Malaysia

25. Maldives

26. Mongolia

27. Myanmar (formerly Burma)

28. Nepal

29. North Korea

30. Oman

31. Pakistan

32 Palestine

33. Philippines

34. Qatar

35. Russia

36. Saudi Arabia

37. Singapore

38. South Korea

39. Sri Lanka

40. Syria

41. Taiwan

42. Tajikistan

43. Thailand

44. Timor-Leste (East Timor)

45. Turkey

46. Turkmenistan

47. United Arab Emirates (UAE)

48. Uzbekistan

49. Vietnam

50. Yemen

72. Countries In South America Answers

1. Argentina
2. Bolivia
3. Brazil

4. Chile

5. Colombia

6. Ecuador

7. Guyana

8. Paraguay

9. Peru

10. Suriname

11. Uruguay

12. Venezuela

13. French Guiana (a department of France, but still considered part of South America)

73. Musical Instruments Answers

1. The violin family's smallest member is the violin.
2. The largest member of the violin family is the double bass.
3. The accordion.
4. The kazoo is a musical instrument that creates a buzzing sound.
5. The bagpipes.
6. The claves.
7. A wind instrument that originated from the Indigenous people of Australia.
8. The trumpet.
9. The maracas.
10. The slide whistle.
11. The cello.
12. The guitar.
13. The piano.
14. The clarinet.
15. The xylophone.
16. The flute.
17. The claves.
18. The harp.
19. The glockenspiel.
20. The tuba.

74. 1960s Bands Answers

1. The Beatles.
2. The Rolling Stones.
3. Jimi Hendrix Experience
4. The Beach Boys.

5. Jim Morrison.
6. The Doors.
7. The Rolling Stones.
8. Steppenwolf.
9. The Jimi Hendrix Experience.
10. Creedence Clearwater Revival.
11. The Mamas & the Papas.
12. The Animals.
13. Sonny & Cher.
14. The Who.
15. Jefferson Airplane.
16. The Lovin' Spoonful.
17. Cream.
18. Buffalo Springfield.
19. The 5th Dimension.
20. The Kinks.

75. 1970s Bands Answers

1. Led Zeppelin
2. Blondie
3. Aerosmith
4. Queen
5. The Clash
6. The Eagles
7. Bee Gees
8. Led Zeppelin
9. The Rolling Stones
10. Boston
11. ABBA
12. The Hollies
13. The Guess Who
14. Pink Floyd
15. Grand Funk Railroad
16. Bee Gees
17. The Knack
18. Queen
19. Lynyrd Skynyrd
20. David Bowie

76. 1980s Bands Answers

1. Van Halen
2. Culture Club
3. Pat Benatar
4. The Cure
5. Motley Crue
6. Toto
7. Queen
8. Bruce Springsteen and the E Street Band
9. U2
10. Devo
11. ZZ Top
12. The Police
13. Guns N' Roses
14. Night Ranger
15. Yes
16. Van Halen
17. Violent Femmes
18. The Smiths

77. 1990s Bands Answers

1. Pearl Jam
2. Radiohead
3. U2
4. Nirvana
5. Green Day
6. Nirvana
7. TLC
8. The Cure
9. Pearl Jam
10. Soundgarden
11. Backstreet Boys
12. 4 Non Blondes
13. Garbage
14. The Smashing Pumpkins
15. Soundgarden
16. Blink-182
17. Live

18. Pearl Jam
19. The Smashing Pumpkins
20. Nirvana

78. 2000s Bands Answers

1. Linkin Park
2. Coldplay
3. The Killers
4. The Killers
5. The Strokes
6. Green Day
7. Arcade Fire
8. Radiohead
9. Interpol
10. Death Cab for Cutie
11. Coldplay
12. Coldplay
13. Snow Patrol
14. The Killers
15. Jimmy Eat World
16. Neutral Milk Hotel
7. The Libertines
18. Modest Mouse
19. Bloc Party
20. Modest Mouse

79. Food Answers

1. Italy
2. Chickpeas
3. Russian
4. Tomatoes, cucumber, onion, feta cheese, and olives.
5. Avocado
6. Parmesan
7. Arborio rice
8. Black pepper
9. Beef and pork
10. Paella
11. Japanese

12. Spaghetti Bolognese
13. Durian
14. Indian
15. Eggplant
16. Eggs
17. Pad Thai
18. Sourdough bread
19. Cheese
20. Pine nuts

80. Desserts Answers

1. Tiramisu
2. Choux pastry
3. Ricotta cheese
4. Meringue
5. Sticky toffee pudding
6. Phyllo dough and nuts (usually walnuts or pistachios)
7. Crème brûlée
8. Apples
9. Cream
10. Churros
11. Key lime pie
12. Fruitcake
13. Ice cream cake
14. Cake
15. Tiramisu
16. Mille-feuille
17. Apple crisp
18. Rasgulla
19. Baklava
20. Dulce de leche.

81. Beers And Where They're From Answers

1. Ireland
2. Netherlands
3. Mexico
4. Belgium
5. United States

6. Germany
7. China
8. Japan
9. Denmark
10/ Turkey
11. Thailand
12. Italy
13. France
14. Philippines
15. Australia
16. México
17. Ireland
18. Singapore
19. Japan
20. Greece
21. Thailand
22. Venezuela
23. Peru
24. Russia
25. Netherlands
26. Belgium
27. England
28. Mexico
29. Jamaica
30. Canada

82. Alcoholic Spirits And Where They're From Answers

1. Mexico
2. Russia
3. Caribbean Islands
4. Scotland
5. United States
6. Ireland
7. France
8. Netherlands
9. Japan
10. Peru
11. France
12. Italy

13/ Korea
14. China
15. Japan
16. France
17. Balkan Peninsula
18. Serbia
19. Scandinavia
20. Mexico
21. Switzerland
22. Greece
23. Turkey
24. Denmark
25. Hungary
26. United Kingdom
27. Netherlands
28. Colombia
29. Argentina
30. Italy

83. Drinks And Their Ingredients Answers

1. Margarita
2. Martini
3. Old Fashioned
4. Manhattan
5. Daiquiri
6. Moscow Mule
7. Mojito
8. Bloody Mary
9. Negroni
10. Cosmopolitan
11. Long Island Iced Tea
12. Mai Tai
13. Sidecar
14. Gin and Tonic
15. Whiskey Sour
16. Pina Colada
17. White Russian
18. Tequila Sunrise
19. Singapore Sling

20. Dark and Stormy

84. Dishes And Where They're From Answers

1. Spain
2. Japan
3. Greece
4. Thailand
5. China
6. Mexico
7. Italy
8. Austria
9. Russia
10. United Kingdom
11. France
12. South Korea
13. Hungary
14. Indonesia
15. India
16. Canada
17. Brazil
18. Middle East
19. Sweden
20. Peru
21. Japan
22. Mexico
23. United Kingdom
24. Turkey
25. Thailand
26. Germany
27. Italy

85. Greek Gods And Their Abilities Answers

1. Zeus
2. Poseidon
3. Hades
4. Hera
5. Athena
6. Apollo

7. Artemis

8. Ares

9. Aphrodite

10. Demeter

11. Hermes

12. Hephaestus

13. Dionysus

14. Hestia

15. Persephone

16. Eros

17. Helios

18. Selene

19. Morpheus

20. Nemesis

86. Roman gods And Their Abilities Answers

1. Jupiter (Jove)

2. Juno

3. Neptune

4. Pluto

5. Venus

6. Mars

7. Mercury

8. Apollo

9. Diana

10. Bacchus (Dionysus)

11. Ceres

12. Vesta

13. Janus

14. Faunus

15. Minerva

16. Proserpina

17. Saturn 1

18. Vulcan

19. Cupid (Eros)

20. Fortuna 2

87. Egyptian Gods And Their Abilities Answers

1. Ra

2. Osiris

3. Isis

4. Horus

5. Anubis

6. Thoth

7. Hathor

8. Sekhmet

9. Set

10. Bastet

88. Cars Answers

1. Ferrari

2. Bayerische Motoren Werke (Bavarian Motor Works)

3. 267 mph

4. Ford

5. Toyota

6. Aufrecht, Melcher and Großaspach (named after the company's founders)

7. Chevrolet

8. Bugatti Chiron Super Sport 300+

9. Sports Utility Vehicle

10. Volkswagen

11. Acura

12. Anti-lock Braking System

13. Ford

14. Model S

15. BMW

16. Honda

17. Revolutions Per Minute

18. Porsche

19. Quattro

20. Mitsubishi

89. Holidays Answers

1. Christmas

2. Halloween

3. Thanksgiving

4. Valentine's Day

5. Independence Day

6. New Year's Day

7. Columbus Day

8. Day of the Dead

9. Labor Day

10. Presidents' Day

11. April Fools' Day

12. Father's Day

13. Mother's Day

14. New Year's Eve

15. Memorial Day

16. Thanksgiving

17. Assumption Day

18. Thanksgiving

19. Flag Day

90. The Internet Answers

1. Hypertext Transfer Protocol.

2. Sir Tim Berners-Lee.

3. Hypertext Markup Language.

4. Mosaic.

5. Search Engine Optimization.

6. "Me at the zoo" by Jawed Karim.

7. "QWERTYUIOP", sent by Ray Tomlinson.

8. Google.

9. Uniform Resource Locator.

10. Six Degrees in 1997.

11. Internet Service Provider.

12. NCSA Mosaic.

13. Domain Name System.

14. Facebook.

15. info.cern.ch.

16. Virtual Private Network.

17. Archie.

18. Internet Protocol.

19. NetMarket.

20. Completely Automated Public Turing test to tell Computers and Humans Apart.

91. Board Games Answers

1. Monopoly
2. Scrabble
3. Battleship
4. Chess
5. Chutes and Ladders
6. Mastermind
7. Checkers
8. Go Fish
9. Go
10. Sorry!
11. Carcassonne
12. Othello
13. Ticket to Ride
14. Checkers
15. Snakes and Ladders
16. Settlers of Catan
17. Rummikub
18. Bluff
19. War
20. Pictionary